RETIREMENT PLANNING SIMPLIFIED

THE COMPLETE TOOLKIT FOR 401K, IRA, AND SMART TAX STRATEGIES TO MAXIMIZE YOUR WEALTH

RETIREWISE

CONTENTS

INTRODUCTION

Welcome to a journey where the path to financial security and peace of mind in your golden years is demystified and made achievable. As we embark on this adventure together, I want you to know that this book is more than just a guide; it's a companion in navigating the often complex world of retirement planning. With a commitment to breaking down intricate financial concepts into understandable, actionable steps, I aim to empower you, the reader, to take control of your future confidently.

This isn't just another retirement planning guide. "Retirement Planning Simplified: The Complete Toolkit for 401K, IRA, and Smart Tax Strategies to Maximize Your Wealth" stands apart by offering a comprehensive approach that marries essential retirement planning tools with real-world applications. From the foundational principles of 401K and IRA accounts to advanced tax strategies and practical examples, each chapter is designed to build upon the last, equipping you with a well-rounded understanding of how to maximize your wealth for a comfortable retirement.

As the third installment in a series that has already explored Social Security, Medicare, Estate, Wills, and Trusts, this book expands upon those crucial topics while focusing on empowering you with the knowledge and tools to plan effectively for retirement. Whether you're familiar with the previous books or are joining us for the first time, you'll find invaluable insights and strategies catering to newcomers and seasoned planners alike.

This book is for you—adults aged 30 and over who may feel overwhelmed by the prospect of retirement planning or are seeking to refine their strategy with innovative, tax-efficient saving solutions. I understand the fears that come with the thought of not having enough saved up or the confusion that complex financial terms and concepts can evoke. That's why I promise to guide you through each step, offering clear, easy-to-follow strategies to help you overcome these hurdles.

Let me encourage you to take charge of your retirement planning journey. Regardless of where you stand today, there is always time to start. This book is designed to inspire, inform, and, most importantly, show you that planning for retirement can be an exciting opportunity to secure the future you envision for yourself and your loved ones.

As we move forward, I urge you to dive into each chapter with an open mind and a commitment to applying the strategies and insights shared. By the end of this book, you will possess a deep understanding of 401K, IRA, and smart tax strategies and a personalized toolkit designed to maximize your wealth for a fulfilling retirement.

The road to retirement planning may seem daunting, but together, we can navigate it with ease and optimism. Let's take this vital step towards securing your financial future.

CHAPTER 1

In the realm of retirement planning, the significance of having a clear and defined vision cannot be overstated. Often, the difference between a future approached with trepidation and one embraced with anticipation lies in the clarity of one's vision for retirement. This chapter delves into the foundational concept of crafting a retirement vision, elucidating why it's beneficial and crucial for effective financial planning.

A well-known adage states, "If you don't know where you're going, any road will get you there." This sentiment rings especially true when it comes to planning for retirement. Without a clear destination in mind, the path becomes ambiguous, and the steps to get there are uncertain. Visualizing your future serves as the compass that guides your retirement planning, ensuring every financial decision aligns with the future you aspire to create.

1.1 THE IMPORTANCE OF A RETIREMENT VISION

Visualizing Your Future

Visualizing your future is akin to setting the destination in your navigational app before starting a journey. It's about defining the endpoint or, in this case, picturing the life you wish to lead once you step away from the workforce. This visualization isn't merely about dreaming; it's a strategic step that lays the groundwork for your retirement planning. By painting a vivid picture of your retirement, including where you'll live, the activities you'll engage in, and the lifestyle you'll lead, you give substance to your goals, making them more tangible and attainable.

Motivation to Save

The direct correlation between having a vivid retirement vision and increased motivation to save and invest for the future is well-documented. Consider the process of saving for a vacation. The excitement of exploring a new destination or revisiting a cherished spot fuels your willingness to set aside funds regularly. Similarly, when you have a vibrant image of your retirement, the motivation to contribute to your retirement funds grows. You're no longer saving for an abstract concept called 'retirement'; you're investing in a future that promises joy, relaxation, and fulfillment.

Customized Planning

A one-size-fits-all approach falls short in retirement planning because each individual's vision of retirement is unique. Some envision a quiet life in a rural setting, surrounded by nature, while others dream of an urban retirement filled with cultural activities and social engagements. Recognizing that your retirement goals require tailored financial strategies is crucial. This realization prompts the customization of your savings and investment plans to suit the specific future you desire. It's about ensuring that your financial strategy is designed with your particular retirement vision in mind, accommodating your expected lifestyle, desired location, and personal aspirations.

Long-term Perspective

Adopting a long-term perspective is essential for making informed, beneficial financial decisions today. It involves looking beyond the immediate gratification of spending to consider the future benefits of saving and investing. This perspective is grounded in the understanding that your actions today significantly impact your future. With a clear retirement vision, it becomes easier to prioritize long-term financial health over short-term pleasures. Saving for retirement becomes a conscious choice to invest in your future self and the life you envisioned.

In essence, creating a retirement vision is not merely an exercise in daydreaming. It's a strategic step in retirement planning that aligns your financial decisions with the future you wish to realize. By clearly visualizing your retirement, you gain the motivation to save, the insight to customize your financial plan, and the wisdom to prioritize long-term gains over immediate satisfaction. This approach ensures that every financial decision is a step towards your envisioned retirement, imbuing your planning efforts with purpose and direction.

1.2 CRAFTING YOUR RETIREMENT VISION

Creating a vision for your retirement is akin to sketching a blueprint for a dream home. Each stroke on the canvas is deliberate, aiming to bring your deepest desires to life. This process requires introspection and a genuine understanding of what happiness means to you in your later years. Here, we explore the facets of life that shape your retirement vision, from personal desires to the legacy you wish to leave behind.

Identifying Your Desires

The first step is to pinpoint what you truly want from your retirement. This part of the process is deeply personal and varies significantly from one individual to another. Some might dream of a quiet life surrounded by nature, while others might envision a retirement filled with adventure and travel. Begin by asking yourself a series of questions to uncover these desires:

- What have I always wanted to do but never had the time for?
- Where do I see myself living?
- How do I want to spend my days?

Your answers will serve as the foundation of your retirement vision and guide your financial planning process. Remember, there are no right or wrong answers here, only what feels true.

Consideration of Lifestyle

Your lifestyle choices, hobbies, and activities shape your retirement vision. These elements determine how you'll spend your time and have financial implications that must be considered. For instance, if you're passionate about travel, your retirement plan should account for the costs associated with your adventures. If you're keen on pursuing hobbies like golf or painting, consider the expenses tied to these interests. Reflect on the following to integrate your lifestyle into your retirement vision:

- The hobbies and activities you wish to pursue
- Any clubs or groups you want to join
- The pace of life you're looking for (e.g., active and busy vs. calm and relaxed)

This reflection ensures your retirement plan supports the lifestyle you aspire to, making your golden years genuinely fulfilling.

Impact of Health on Retirement

Health is a pivotal factor that influences your retirement planning, often dictating the activities you can partake in and the care you might require. It's essential to assess your current and potential future health considerations. This assessment helps create a retirement plan that accommodates healthcare costs, insurance, and any necessary adjustments to your living situation. Key considerations include:

- Your current health status and any ongoing medical needs
- Family health history and potential future health concerns
- Health insurance coverage and options for long-term care

By factoring in health considerations, you ensure your retirement plan is robust, adaptive, and capable of supporting you through various health scenarios.

Family and Legacy Aspirations

Finally, consider the role of family, community, and the legacy you wish to create in shaping your retirement vision. For many, retirement provides an opportunity to strengthen family bonds, contribute to the community, and leave a lasting impact. Reflect on the following to incorporate these aspects into your retirement vision:

- The kind of relationship you wish to have with your family and friends
- Any community service or philanthropic work you want to be involved in
- The legacy you hope to leave behind, whether through financial means, education, or other forms of support

This contemplation ensures your retirement plan caters to your personal and lifestyle needs and aligns with your broader aspirations for family and legacy.

In crafting your retirement vision, it's vital to weave together these diverse threads—from personal desires and lifestyle choices to health considerations and family aspirations. This holistic approach ensures your retirement plan is not just a financial strategy but a blueprint for a fulfilling and meaningful future.

1.3 ALIGNING YOUR FINANCIAL GOALS WITH YOUR VISION

Once you have a vivid picture of your desired retirement, the next step is to translate this vision into concrete, achievable financial goals. This process is akin to charting a course on a map. You know your destination and must plot the waypoints to get there. Aligning your financial goals with your retirement vision requires specificity, prioritization, flexibility, and a commitment to regular reassessment.

Setting Measurable Goals

Setting specific, measurable goals is the first step in aligning your financial goals with your retirement vision. This specificity is what turns vague aspirations into actionable targets. For example, instead of the broad goal of "saving enough for retirement," a measurable goal would be "saving $1 million by age 65." This specificity provides clarity and a target to aim for.

- Break it down: Start by breaking down your retirement vision into aspects that require financial backing. Consider housing, daily living costs, healthcare, travel, hobbies, and family commitments.
- Quantify your needs: Estimate the financial resources needed for each aspect of your vision. Use online calculators or consult with a financial advisor to help quantify these needs.
- Set time frames: Assign a time frame to each goal. Knowing when you want to retire influences how much you need to

save each year, adjusting for factors like investment growth and inflation.

Prioritizing Your Goals

With various components comprising your retirement vision, prioritizing your financial goals becomes crucial. It's about understanding that not all goals can simultaneously be pursued equally, especially when resources are limited.

- Essential vs. desirable: Categorize your goals into 'essential' and 'desirable.' Essentials are non-negotiable goals for retirement, such as healthcare funding and basic living expenses. Desirables might include travel or luxury items.
- Short-term vs. long-term: Some goals need immediate attention, while others are for the long term. Prioritizing helps in managing current financial pressures without losing sight of future objectives.
- Cost-benefit analysis: Assess the impact of each goal on your overall vision. Goals that significantly enhance your retirement happiness might take precedence over those with less impact.

Flexible Planning

Flexibility in planning acknowledges that life is unpredictable. Changes in health, economic conditions, or personal circumstances can affect your retirement vision and the financial goals aligned with it. Incorporating flexibility ensures your plan remains viable, no matter what life throws your way.

- Build in a buffer: When estimating the financial needs for your goals, consider adding a buffer to account for unforeseen expenses or economic changes. A buffer enhances your plan's resilience to shocks.

- Diversify your investments: A diversified portfolio can provide more stable returns and protect against market volatility. This stability supports your financial goals amidst changing economic landscapes.
- Adjustable goals: Be prepared to revise your goals based on life changes. For instance, a health setback might prioritize healthcare savings over leisure travel.

Review and Adjust

A critical aspect of aligning your financial goals with your retirement vision is the commitment to regularly review and adjust your goals. This process ensures that your plan evolves along with your life circumstances and retirement vision.

- Annual reviews: Set aside time each year to review your financial goals and the progress you've made towards them. This review should consider changes in your personal life, economic conditions, and any shifts in your retirement vision.
- Adjust contributions: Based on your annual review, you may need to increase or decrease your savings contributions. Adjusting contributions keeps you on track to meet your goals within the set time frames.
- Reassess risk tolerance: As you approach retirement, reassessing your risk tolerance is crucial. Shifting towards more conservative investments can protect your nest egg from market downturns as you near your retirement date.

Aligning your financial goals with your retirement vision is an ongoing process, not a one-time task. It's a dynamic strategy requiring regular attention and adjustments to ensure you continuously move toward your desired future. This approach not only keeps your retirement plans realistic and achievable but also provides peace of mind, knowing that you're actively steering your financial ship toward the retirement of your dreams.

Navigating this process requires dedication, foresight, and sometimes willingness to make tough decisions. However, the reward is a retirement that closely matches your vision, crafted through thoughtful planning and informed by a deep understanding of your personal aspirations and financial realities.

2

DEMYSTIFYING RETIREMENT ACCOUNTS: 401K AND IRA DECODED

I magine standing at the base of a mountain, gazing up at the peak. You're about to climb, not with gear and ropes, but with knowledge and strategies—your tools for scaling the financial heights of retirement planning. Now, think of 401K and IRA accounts as two distinct paths up the mountain. Both lead to the summit—your secure retirement—but each offers different views and challenges. This chapter aims to clear the fog around these paths, making your climb smoother.

2.1 DEMYSTIFYING 401K AND IRA: WHAT YOU NEED TO KNOW

Understanding the basics

Before you set foot on either path, let's get familiar with the terrain. A 401K is often introduced through your workplace, offering a convenient way to save for retirement directly from your paycheck. Think of it as a savings account with a twist: the money you contribute is invested, allowing it to grow over time. On the other hand, an Individual Retirement Account (IRA) is something you set up on your own. It's like opening a personal savings account for retirement, with the freedom to invest in a broader range of options.

- 401K accounts typically come with an employer match, which is akin to free money towards your retirement. If your employer offers a match, try contributing at least enough to get the full match; it's an instant return on your investment.
- IRA accounts offer more investment choices than most 401K plans, allowing you to tailor your retirement savings more closely to your personal preferences and financial goals.

Contribution limits and rules

The IRS limits how much you can contribute to these accounts each year. For 2021, the limit for 401K contributions is $19,500, with an additional catch-up contribution of $6,500 if you're 50 or older. IRAs have lower limits: $6,000 per year, with an additional $1,000 for those 50 and up. These limits can change, so it's vital to stay updated.

- Tax treatment is a key difference between these accounts. Contributions to a traditional 401K or IRA can reduce your taxable income in the year you make them, potentially lowering your tax bill. However, you'll pay taxes on withdrawals in retirement.

Choosing between Roth and Traditional

Imagine you're at a fork in the road: one path is labeled "Traditional" and the other "Roth." With Traditional accounts, you get a tax break up front, leading to immediate savings. Roth accounts, however, flip the script. You pay taxes on your contributions now, but withdrawals in retirement are tax-free.

- For a Roth account, think about your current and future tax situation. If you expect to be in a higher tax bracket in retirement, paying taxes now might make more sense. The Roth option is like paying for all your mountain climbing gear upfront, knowing you won't have to worry about any costs when you reach the summit.
- For a Traditional account, it's beneficial if you anticipate being in a lower tax bracket in retirement than you are now. You defer taxes until retirement, potentially reducing your tax liability when your income may be lower.

Withdrawal rules and penalties

Understanding when and how you can access your money is crucial. For both 401K and IRA accounts, you're generally allowed to start making penalty-free withdrawals at age 59½. Withdraw too early, and you could face a 10% penalty on top of regular income taxes. However, some exceptions might allow you to tap into these funds early without penalty, such as certain medical expenses or a first-time home purchase.

- Required Minimum Distributions (RMDs) are another critical aspect. Once you reach age 72, the IRS requires you to take minimum withdrawals from your traditional 401K and IRA accounts. Roth IRAs are exempt from RMDs during the owner's lifetime, making them a flexible tool for managing your retirement income and tax situation.
- Visual Aid: Consider including a chart that compares Traditional and Roth accounts side by side, highlighting contribution limits, tax treatment, withdrawal rules, and RMD requirements. This visual could serve as a quick reference for readers to understand the differences at a glance.
- Interactive Element: A quiz titled "Which Retirement Account is Right for You?" could help readers assess their current

financial situation, tax considerations, and retirement goals to guide them toward the type of account that might best suit their needs.

Both 401K and IRA accounts are powerful tools in your retirement planning toolkit. By understanding the basics, contribution limits and rules, and the differences between Roth and Traditional options, you're better equipped to make informed decisions that align with your retirement vision. Remember, choosing the right path depends on your goals, tax situation, and investment preferences. As you climb towards financial security in retirement, remember these insights to navigate the terrain confidently.

2.2 ROTH VS. TRADITIONAL: MAKING SENSE OF YOUR CHOICES

In the landscape of retirement savings, selecting between Roth and Traditional accounts is akin to choosing the right gear for your climb. Both have distinct features and benefits, shaped mainly by tax implications, eligibility requirements, and their potential impact on long-term financial health. This section aims to demystify these options, providing insights to help you align your choice with your financial goals and circumstances.

Tax Implications

At the heart of the Roth versus Traditional debate lies their differing tax treatments. With Traditional accounts, your contributions are made pre-tax, reducing your annual taxable income. This immediate tax benefit can be particularly advantageous if you're in a higher tax bracket. However, when retirement comes, and you start withdrawing funds, those distributions are taxed as ordinary income. This deferred tax can be a double-edged sword, depending on your income level in retirement.

Roth accounts, conversely, offer a reverse tax scenario. Contributions are made with after-tax dollars, meaning there's no immediate tax deduction. The magic happens in retirement—withdrawals, including earnings, are tax-free, provided certain conditions are met. This can be a significant advantage, especially if you expect to be in a higher tax bracket in retirement or if tax rates rise across the board.

- Immediate vs. future tax benefits: Traditional accounts may offer a tax break today, while Roth accounts promise tax-free income in retirement.

Eligibility Requirements

Not everyone can freely choose between Roth and Traditional IRAs due to income eligibility requirements, particularly for Roth IRAs. For those with higher incomes, there may be limits to how much can be contributed to a Roth IRA, or they may not be eligible to contribute at all. Traditional IRAs, on the other hand, don't have these income restrictions for contributions. However, there are limits on the deductibility of contributions if a retirement plan at work covers you or your spouse.

- Roth IRA income limits: For individuals and couples exceeding certain income thresholds, Roth IRA contributions may be reduced or not allowed.
- Traditional IRA deductibility: If a workplace retirement plan covers you, your ability to deduct Traditional IRA contributions on your taxes may be limited based on your income.

Long-term Benefits

When evaluating Roth and Traditional accounts, consider the long-term implications of each choice. A Roth IRA can be particularly compelling if you anticipate needing flexibility with your withdrawals in retirement. Unlike Traditional IRAs, Roth IRAs do not require minimum distributions starting at age 72, allowing your savings to grow tax-free if you don't need to access them. This can significantly benefit estate planning, enabling you to leave tax-free money to your heirs.

Traditional IRA funds are taxed at your income tax rate when withdrawn in retirement. If your tax rate is lower in retirement than during your working years, this can work in your favor. However, required minimum distributions (RMDs) from these accounts can push you into a higher tax bracket, affecting your overall tax situation.

- Withdrawal flexibility: Roth IRAs offer more flexibility, with tax-free withdrawals and no RMDs, which can benefit estate planning.
- Tax rate considerations: If you anticipate a lower tax rate in retirement, Traditional accounts could offer more benefits in the long run.

Case Studies

To illustrate the impact of choosing between Roth and Traditional accounts, consider two hypothetical case studies:

- Case Study 1: Alex, age 30, expects her career trajectory to significantly increase her income over time. She opts for a Roth IRA, contributing $6,000 annually. By retirement at 65, assuming a 7% annual return, her account grows to over $1 million, with all withdrawals tax-free, offering a substantial benefit given her higher expected tax bracket in retirement.
- Case Study 2: Jordan, also 30, is currently in a high tax bracket but expects a more modest income in retirement. He chooses a Traditional IRA for the immediate tax deduction,

contributing $6,000 annually. At a 7% return, his account also grows to over $1 million by age 65. However, his withdrawals are taxed as ordinary income. Assuming a lower tax bracket in retirement, Jordan still benefits from significant tax savings.

These case studies underscore the importance of aligning your retirement account choice with your financial situation and expectations for the future. While Roth IRAs offer tax-free growth and withdrawals, their benefits are maximized when you expect to be in a higher tax bracket in retirement. With their tax-deferred growth and contributions, traditional IRAs can be advantageous if you anticipate being in a lower tax bracket when you retire.

2.3 UNDERSTANDING ASSET ALLOCATION AND DIVERSIFICATION

Asset allocation and diversification play pivotal roles in retirement savings. When applied thoughtfully, these strategies are the backbone of effective risk management and instrumental in steering you toward your retirement objectives. This section will illuminate how these strategies mitigate investment risk and ensure your portfolio aligns with your evolving retirement vision.

Risk Management

Asset allocation involves dividing your investment portfolio among different asset categories—stocks, bonds, and cash being the most common. This strategy is fundamental for managing investment risk because different asset classes respond differently to market conditions. While stocks offer high growth potential, they come with increased volatility. Bonds, on the other hand, typically provide more stable returns. Cash, or cash equivalents like money market funds, offer the lowest risk and potential returns.

Balancing these asset categories to reflect your risk tolerance and investment timeline is key to effective risk management. For instance, if market fluctuations keep you awake at night, you might lean towards a higher allocation in bonds and cash. Conversely, if you're comfortable with short-term market swings in exchange for potential long-term growth, a higher stock allocation could be more your speed.

Achieving Your Retirement Vision

Diversification, or spreading your investments across various assets, further refines the concept of asset allocation. It's about not putting all your eggs in one basket. Within each asset category, you can diversify further—by investing in a mix of sectors, industries, and geographies. This approach can cushion your portfolio against significant losses if one investment or market segment underperforms.

Proper diversification is aligned closely with achieving your retirement goals. It allows for the potential growth needed to reach your objectives while mitigating risk to a comfortable level. For example, if part of your vision involves traveling extensively, ensuring your portfolio has growth potential through diversified equity investments can help fund those dreams. At the same time, maintaining a portion of your portfolio in more stable investments provides a safety net.

Balancing Your Portfolio

Maintaining balance in your investment portfolio is an ongoing process. Over time, market movements can cause your initial asset allocation to shift, potentially exposing you to more risk than intended or skewing your investments away from your retirement goals. Regularly reviewing and rebalancing your portfolio ensures it stays aligned with your strategic asset allocation.

The rebalancing process might involve selling investments that have grown to constitute a more significant portion of your portfolio than desired and buying more of those that now make up less. This disciplined approach forces you to "buy low and sell high," contributing to the potential for solid long-term returns.

Age-Based Allocation Strategies

As you approach retirement, adjusting your asset allocation becomes increasingly important. In your early working years, a higher proportion of stocks might be appropriate, capitalizing on their growth potential over a longer period. However, as retirement approaches, gradually shifting towards bonds and cash equivalents can help preserve your accumulated wealth.

This doesn't mean shifting entirely out of stocks. Maintaining a portion of your portfolio in equities can still be beneficial, providing growth potential to counteract inflation and extend the longevity of your savings. Age-based allocation strategies offer a structured approach to gradually decrease investment risk as you age, keeping your portfolio in tune with your changing risk tolerance and time horizon.

By embracing asset allocation and diversification, you create a robust framework for your retirement savings. This strategic approach manages risk and propels you towards your retirement aspirations. It's about finding the right balance that matches your risk tolerance with your long-term goals, ensuring your investment strategy evolves alongside your life's journey.

Remember what we've discussed as we wrap up this exploration of asset allocation and diversification. These strategies are about more than just numbers and allocations; they're about crafting a pathway that leads to the retirement you envision. Balancing risk and growth, ensuring your investments reflect your goals, and adjusting your approach as you age are all critical steps.

Looking ahead, staying informed, and making educated decisions about your retirement planning cannot be overstated. Our journey continues as we delve deeper into the intricacies of retirement planning, equipping you with the knowledge and tools needed to navigate the complexities of this critical life stage. Your proactive engagement with these concepts lays the groundwork for a retirement filled with the fulfillment of your dreams and goals.

3

LAYING THE FINANCIAL
FOUNDATION FOR RETIREMENT

I magine you're setting out to build your dream home. Before the first brick is laid, you need a clear blueprint and a solid foundation. Similarly, a secure retirement rests on understanding your current financial situation. This chapter is your guide to conducting a personal financial audit, an essential step to ensure your retirement planning is built on solid ground.

A personal financial audit provides a snapshot of where you stand financially. It's like a financial health check-up, highlighting areas of strength and those needing attention. This process is critical for anyone looking to make informed decisions about their retirement planning. Let's dive into how you can conduct your own financial audit, starting with listing your assets and liabilities, understanding your cash flow, identifying your financial strengths and weaknesses, and setting the stage for improvement.

Listing Assets and Liabilities

The first step in a financial audit is to list all your assets (what you own) and liabilities (what you owe). This might sound straightforward, but it's essential to be thorough.

Assets include:

- Savings and checking accounts
- Retirement accounts (401K, IRA)
- Real estate
- Investments (stocks, bonds, mutual funds)
- Personal property (vehicles, jewelry)

Liabilities include:

- Mortgage
- Car loans
- Credit card debt
- Student loans
- Other personal loans

Creating a detailed list gives you a clear picture of your net worth. It's like taking inventory before a big move; you need to know what you have and what's weighing you down.

Understanding Your Cash Flow

Next, it's time to analyze your income and expenses. This step tracks how much money comes in and where it goes each month.

Start by listing all sources of income, including:

- Salary
- Rental income
- Interest and dividends
- Any other earnings

Then, categorize your expenses. Common categories include:

- Housing (rent or mortgage)
- Utilities
- Groceries
- Transportation
- Insurance premiums
- Entertainment
- Savings and investments

This exercise helps you identify spending patterns and areas to cut back. It's akin to reviewing your grocery list to see where you can save money without compromising quality.

Identifying Financial Strengths and Weaknesses

With a clear understanding of your assets, liabilities, and cash flow, you can now identify your financial strengths and areas for improvement. Strengths might include a robust emergency fund or a well-diversified investment portfolio. Weaknesses could be high levels of debt or insufficient savings for future goals.

This process is like a coach reviewing game footage. It's about understanding what strategies are working and where adjustments are needed to improve performance.

Setting the Stage for Improvement

With this knowledge, you can start making impactful changes toward your retirement goals. This might involve increasing your savings rate, paying down debt, or reallocating your investments. The key is to create a plan of action that moves you closer to your ideal retirement.

Consider setting SMART goals (Specific, Measurable, Achievable, Relevant, Time-bound) for each area you'd like to improve. For example, rather than a vague goal like "save more money," a SMART goal would be "increase monthly savings by $200 for the next 12 months."

3.1 TOOLS AND RESOURCES TO ASSIST YOUR AUDIT

- Budgeting apps can automate much of the work involved in tracking income and expenses. Many apps link directly to your financial accounts, categorizing transactions in real time.
- Net worth trackers help you monitor your assets and liabilities, giving you an instant view of your financial health.
- Debt repayment calculators offer strategies for efficiently paying down liabilities, showing how changing payment amounts or frequencies can impact your overall interest paid.

Interactive Element: Financial Audit Checklist

A comprehensive checklist can ensure you recognize all assets and liabilities during your audit. This tool simplifies the process, guiding you through each step and helping you organize your financial information effectively.

- Assets: List all checking and savings accounts, retirement accounts, other investments, real estate, and valuable personal property.
- Liabilities: Detail all mortgages, car loans, student loans, credit card debt, and other personal loans.
- Income: Record all sources of monthly income, including salary, rental income, and any other earnings.
- Expenses: Categorize monthly expenses, including housing, utilities, groceries, transportation, insurance, entertainment, and savings.

This checklist serves as a roadmap for your financial audit, ensuring a thorough examination of your current financial situation. By completing each section, you lay the groundwork for informed, strategic retirement planning.

Setting the stage for improvement involves taking proactive steps based on the insights gained from your financial audit. It's about making choices today that align with your long-term retirement vision, ensuring that when the time comes, you're ready to build your dream retirement brick by brick.

3.2 CALCULATING YOUR NET WORTH FOR RETIREMENT PLANNING

Understanding your net worth is like having a financial compass that points you toward your retirement goals. It's a measure of what you own minus what you owe, providing a clear snapshot of your financial health at any given time. This clarity is indispensable for making informed decisions about your retirement planning.

Defining Net Worth

At its core, net worth encapsulates the value of all your assets after subtracting your liabilities. Assets can be anything from savings accounts, retirement funds, investments, and personal property like your home or car. Liabilities include mortgages, loans, and any other debts. The equation is straightforward: Assets - Liabilities = Net Worth. Yet, its implications for your financial strategy are profound, serving as a litmus test for your fiscal well-being.

Importance of Knowing Your Net Worth

Pinpointing your net worth is not merely about crunching numbers; it's about laying the groundwork for a secure future. This figure acts as a benchmark, helping you assess whether you're on track to meet your retirement objectives or if adjustments are needed. A positive and growing net worth indicates financial stability and progress toward your goals. At the same time, a stagnant or negative figure might signal the need for a strategic pivot in your financial planning.

Steps to Calculate Net Worth

Calculating your net worth involves a few straightforward steps:

1. List all assets: Start by making a comprehensive list of your assets. Include everything from liquid assets like cash in checking and savings accounts to retirement accounts (401K, IRA), other investments, and valuable personal property. Remember to appraise items like your home or vehicles at market value.
2. Tally up liabilities: Next, list all your liabilities. This includes the remaining balance on your mortgage, car loans, student loans, credit card debt, and any other money you owe.
3. Subtract liabilities from assets: With both totals in hand, subtract your total liabilities from your total assets. The result is your net worth.
4. Review and adjust: This calculation isn't a one-time task; it's something you should do regularly. As your financial situation evolves, so too will your net worth. Regular reviews help you stay aligned with your retirement goals.

Using Net Worth as a Planning Tool

Your net worth isn't just a number; it's a tool that can guide your financial strategy. Here's how you can use it effectively:

- Set benchmarks: Use your net worth as a benchmark to gauge your financial progress over time. Regularly tracking this figure can motivate you to increase your assets and decrease your liabilities, pushing you closer to your retirement goals.
- Assess financial health: A comprehensive view of your net worth allows you to evaluate your financial health. It shows

where you stand today and helps identify areas needing more attention, whether boosting your savings, investing more aggressively, or paying down debt.

- Inform decision-making: When faced with financial decisions, your net worth provides a clear reference point. It can help determine if you're in a position to make significant financial moves, such as purchasing a home, investing in property, or even retiring early.
- Strategic adjustments: If your net worth isn't where you want it to be, knowing your exact financial position allows you to make strategic adjustments to your savings and investment plans. This might mean reallocating assets to more productive investments, finding ways to increase income, or implementing a more aggressive debt reduction strategy.

Calculating and understanding your net worth is a vital step in retirement planning. It offers a precise, quantitative measure of your financial health, guiding your journey towards a secure and fulfilling retirement. By regularly assessing your net worth, you can make informed decisions that bring you closer to achieving your financial and retirement goals.

3.3 SETTING UP YOUR EMERGENCY FUND: A PRE-RETIREMENT MUST

An emergency fund is a financial safety net designed to cover unexpected expenses without derailing your long-term financial plans. In retirement planning, this fund takes on an even greater significance. It serves as a buffer against unforeseen costs and ensures that your retirement savings continue to grow, uninterrupted by life's unpredictable events.

Why You Need an Emergency Fund

Life is full of surprises, some less welcome than others. Medical emergencies, sudden home repairs, or unexpected job loss can stress your finances. Without an emergency fund, you might be forced to dip into your retirement savings or take on high-interest debt to cover these costs. This fund acts as a protective barrier, safeguarding your retirement plans from short-term upheavals.

Determining the Size of Your Fund

The size of your emergency fund should reflect your unique circumstances, considering your monthly expenses, job stability, and the number of income earners in your household. A general guideline is to have three to six months' worth of living expenses saved. However, if your job situation is less stable or you're the sole income provider, aiming for a larger fund—perhaps up to a year's worth of expenses—might be prudent.

To calculate the size of your fund:

- Tally your monthly essential expenses, including housing, utilities, groceries, and insurance.
- Multiply this total by the number of months you aim to cover (between three and twelve, depending on your situation).
- Consider adding a buffer for additional peace of mind.

Best Practices for Managing Your Fund

Where and how you store your emergency fund can significantly impact its effectiveness. The fund should be easily accessible but not so easy that you're tempted to use it for non-emergencies. High-yield savings accounts or money market accounts are excellent choices. They offer better interest rates than traditional savings accounts while providing the liquidity you need to withdraw funds quickly in an emergency.

When managing your emergency fund:

- Keep it separate from your daily checking account to avoid the temptation to dip into it for everyday expenses.
- Regularly review and adjust the fund size as your living expenses or income changes.
- Automate contributions to your emergency fund to ensure it continues to grow.

Integrating Your Fund with Your Overall Retirement Plan

An emergency fund is not just another account; it's an integral component of your broader retirement planning strategy. It supports your long-term goals by providing a financial cushion, allowing your investments to remain untouched and continue compounding. Additionally, this fund can give you the confidence to invest more aggressively in your retirement accounts, knowing you have a safety net for short-term needs.

Incorporating your emergency fund into your retirement strategy involves:

- Regularly reassess your fund size in the context of your overall retirement plan to ensure it remains aligned with your changing financial landscape.
- Considering the role of your emergency fund in your asset allocation, particularly as you approach retirement, your risk tolerance may decrease.
- Using your emergency fund as a buffer to avoid premature withdrawals from retirement accounts, which can incur penalties and set back your retirement progress.

A well-planned emergency fund is more than just a financial safe-guard; it's a cornerstone of a resilient retirement strategy. It ensures that when faced with life's inevitable surprises, you have the resources to manage without compromising your long-term financial well-being. By carefully determining the size of your fund, choosing the right place to keep it, and seamlessly integrating it with your retirement planning, you create a comprehensive approach that supports both your present and future financial security.

As this chapter concludes, remember that an emergency fund is not optional but a fundamental element of your retirement planning. It acts as your first line of defense against life's unpredictability, ensuring that your plans for a secure, comfortable retirement remain on track regardless of what comes your way. Moving forward, the insights you've gained here will serve as a solid foundation for building a comprehensive retirement strategy that not only withstands life's storms but thrives in anticipation of the sunny days ahead.

4

MAXIMIZING YOUR RETIREMENT POTENTIAL

In the tapestry of retirement planning, few threads are as vibrant and crucial as understanding the power of compounding. It's a simple concept with profound implications, yet it often flies under the radar, overshadowed by more immediate financial concerns. This chapter sheds light on this financial phenomenon, revealing how it can significantly amplify your retirement savings.

4.1 THE POWER OF COMPOUNDING IN YOUR RETIREMENT ACCOUNTS

Understanding Compounding

Compounding is about earning interest on your interest, creating a snowball effect that can substantially grow your retirement savings over time. It's akin to planting a tree. Initially, the growth seems slow, but given time, that same tree sprawls out, providing shade far beyond its original size. Similarly, even modest contributions to your retirement accounts can expand exponentially through compounding, provided they have sufficient time to grow.

Start Saving Early

The secret to harnessing the full potential of compounding lies in starting early. The sooner you begin saving, the more time your money has to work for you. Consider two savers: one starts contributing to their retirement account at 25, while the other waits until 35. Even if the latter saves more money overall, the early starter often comes out ahead by retirement, thanks to the extra decade of compounding growth. This emphasizes the importance of saving and starting as soon as possible.

Reinvesting Dividends and Interest

For compounding to truly take effect, reinvesting dividends and interest is crucial. Instead of pocketing these earnings, funneling them back into your retirement account allows them to contribute to the compounding process. It's like adding more snow to your snowball; the more you add, the bigger it grows. This strategy requires discipline but can significantly increase the size of your retirement nest egg over time.

Real-Life Examples

To illustrate the power of compounding, let's look at an actual scenario involving a retirement savings account. Imagine starting with a $5,000 investment and contributing an additional $200 monthly. With an average annual return of 7%, your investment would grow to over $263,000 in 30 years. Without adding to the initial investment, that $5,000 alone would grow to nearly $40,000 in the same timeframe, showcasing compounding's ability to multiply your savings.

Visual Element: Infographics on Compounding

An infographic titled "The Magic of Compounding" could visually show how a consistent, modest investment can grow over different periods, highlighting the impact of early and continued contributions versus starting later in life.

Interactive Element: Compounding Calculator Exercise

A compounding calculator exercise could engage readers by allowing them to input their savings information—starting balance, monthly contribution, expected annual return, and time frame—to see first-hand how their retirement savings could grow. This real-time interaction makes the concept of compounding more tangible. It personalizes it, showing the potential growth of their specific investments.

Textual Element: Reflection Section on Financial Habits

A reflection section could invite readers to assess their current savings habits and consider adjustments to better leverage compounding. Questions might include:

- How early did I start saving for retirement?
- Do I regularly reinvest dividends and interest?
- What changes can I make to maximize the benefits of compounding in my retirement planning?

By directly engaging with these concepts, readers can better understand the importance of early and consistent saving, the benefits of reinvesting earnings, and the tangible impact these strategies can have on their retirement savings. Through real-life examples, interactive exercises, and personal reflection, this chapter aims to transform the abstract concept of compounding into a concrete, actionable strategy for maximizing retirement potential.

4.2 CATCH-UP CONTRIBUTIONS: IT'S NEVER TOO LATE TO START

In retirement savings, a provision exists that acts like a second wind for those who find themselves behind in their journey toward financial security. This provision, known as catch-up contributions, addresses the concerns of individuals 50 or older, offering them an opportunity to accelerate their savings as they approach retirement. This section highlights what catch-up contributions entail, who is eligible, and how they can significantly bolster your retirement savings.

Defining Catch-Up Contributions and Eligibility

Catch-up contributions allow individuals aged 50 and above to contribute additional funds beyond the standard limits to their retirement accounts, such as 401Ks and IRAs. This is particularly beneficial for those who might not have saved enough in their earlier years or wish to maximize their savings in the final stretch before retirement. The government updates these contribution limits annually, so staying informed on the latest figures is crucial.

Strategies for Making Catch-Up Contributions

Several strategies can enhance the impact of catch-up contributions on retirement savings for those eligible.

- Maximize Contributions: First and foremost, if financially feasible, maximize your catch-up contributions each year. This might mean adjusting your budget to allocate more to your retirement accounts. Still, the potential payoff in terms of additional savings can be substantial.
- Focus on High-Interest Accounts: Consider directing your catch-up contributions to accounts with higher growth potential. While this might involve a higher risk, the potential

for increased returns can significantly improve your retirement savings over time.

- Tax Considerations: Evaluate the tax implications of contributing to different types of retirement accounts. For example, contributions to a traditional IRA might offer immediate tax deductions, whereas contributions to a Roth IRA provide tax-free withdrawals in retirement.
- Professional Advice: Consult with a financial advisor to tailor a catch-up contribution strategy that aligns with your retirement plan and financial situation. A personalized approach can help identify the most effective way to leverage catch-up contributions for your specific needs.

Impact on Retirement Savings

The effect of catch-up contributions on your retirement savings can be profound. By taking advantage of this opportunity, you can significantly close the savings gap if you started saving later in life or enhance your existing nest egg. The additional contributions compound over time, potentially increasing your retirement savings by tens or even hundreds of thousands of dollars, depending on how much and how long you contribute.

Motivational Success Stories

Consider the stories of individuals who have successfully utilized catch-up contributions to enhance their retirement savings to illustrate the real-world impact.

- Case Study 1: Sarah began focusing on her retirement savings at 50, feeling concerned that she hadn't saved enough. By maximizing her catch-up contributions annually and focusing on high-growth investment options, she was able to significantly increase her retirement fund, giving her the financial security she sought for her retirement years.

- Case Study 2: Mark, at 55, realized he was not on track to retire comfortably. He consulted with a financial advisor and adjusted his budget to maximize his catch-up contributions to both his 401K and IRA. By the time he retired at 67, these strategic contributions had added over $150,000 to his retirement savings, significantly improving his retirement lifestyle.

These stories underscore that enhancing your retirement savings is never too late. With the right strategy and a commitment to maximizing catch-up contributions, you can make meaningful progress toward your retirement goals, regardless of when you started saving.

Catch-up contributions are a powerful tool for those looking to boost their retirement savings later in life. Whether you're playing catch-up or simply aiming to fortify your nest egg, taking full advantage of these contributions can have a lasting impact on your financial well-being in retirement. By understanding and strategically employing catch-up contributions, you allow yourself to secure the retirement you envision, filled with the freedom and peace of mind that financial stability brings.

4.3 EMPLOYER MATCH: MAXIMIZING FREE MONEY

Grasping Employer Match Programs

In the landscape of retirement savings, employer match programs stand out as pivotal benefits that can significantly enhance your financial readiness for retirement. These programs, offered with 401(k) plans and sometimes other retirement accounts, involve your employer contributing a certain amount to your retirement savings plan based on the amount you contribute, up to a certain percentage of your salary. It's akin to receiving a bonus that grows over time, a reward for your foresight in saving for the future.

Pinpointing Optimal Contribution Rates

To fully benefit from an employer match program, you must contribute enough from your paycheck to trigger the maximum match from your employer. This optimal rate varies but is often expressed as a percentage of your salary. For instance, if your employer offers a 100% match on the first 3% of your salary that you contribute, you should aim to contribute at least that 3%. Failing to do so leaves money on the table. A straightforward approach to calculating this is to review your pay stubs and employer's plan documentation to understand the match formula and adjust your contribution rate accordingly.

Sidestepping Common Pitfalls

While employer match programs are lucrative, employees often commit several avoidable mistakes. Not contributing enough to get the full match, delaying participation in the plan, or not increasing contributions as salaries rise can all diminish the potential benefits. Another common oversight is not comprehensively understanding the vesting schedule, which dictates when the employer-matched funds become entirely yours. Staying informed and proactive can help you navigate these pitfalls, maximizing the benefit.

Advocating for Enhanced Benefits

Negotiating better retirement benefits, including improved employer match rates, is seldom approached by employees but can be a fruitful discussion. Preparation is key; arm yourself with knowledge of standard practices in your industry and present a reasoned case to your HR department or management. Highlighting the mutual benefits of enhanced retirement contributions, such as increased employee retention and satisfaction, can bolster your argument. Remember, negotiations should be approached with tact and an understanding of your employer's perspective.

As we conclude this section, it's crucial to remember the value of employer match programs as part of your retirement planning strategy. By understanding how these programs work, calculating the optimal contribution rates, avoiding common mistakes, and even negotiating for better terms, you're positioning yourself for a more secure financial future. Each step you take strengthens the foundation of your retirement savings, bringing you closer to realizing your goals for a comfortable and fulfilling retirement.

Moving forward, the insights gained here serve as building blocks for more advanced strategies in retirement planning. Each decision you make, from how much to contribute to your retirement accounts to how you negotiate your benefits, is critical in shaping your financial landscape for the years to come.

5

SMART INVESTMENT CHOICES FOR RETIREMENT

I magine walking into an art gallery where the walls are adorned with a myriad of paintings. Each artwork's distinct style and color palette contributes to the gallery's overall appeal. This variety isn't just visually pleasing; it's essential, ensuring that every visitor finds something that resonates. Similarly, building a diversified retirement portfolio involves mixing various investment types to meet your financial goals. This chapter will guide you through this process, akin to curating your financial gallery, ensuring it reflects your unique needs and aspirations.

5.1 BUILDING A DIVERSIFIED PORTFOLIO: A BEGINNER'S GUIDE

Principles of diversification

Diversification is a strategy that involves spreading your investments across various assets to reduce risk. Think of it as not putting all your eggs in one basket. If one investment performs poorly, you're less likely to see a significant impact on your entire portfolio because other investments might perform well, balancing out the overall performance. This principle is crucial for retirement investing because it aims to achieve a smoother ride over the long term, mitigating the ups and downs of the market.

Asset classes overview

A well-diversified portfolio includes a mix of asset classes. Here's a brief overview:

- Stocks: Represent shares in companies. While they can be volatile, they also offer high growth potential over the long term.
- Bonds: Loans made to corporations or governments that pay back with interest. They are generally less risky than stocks and offer regular income.
- Cash and cash equivalents: These include savings accounts and money market funds. They are the least risky assets but provide lower returns.
- Real estate: These can be direct investments in property or through real estate investment trusts (REITs). Real estate can provide income and potential appreciation.
- Commodities: Such as gold, oil, and agricultural products. They can be a hedge against inflation but are subject to market fluctuations.

Diversification strategies

To create a diversified portfolio, consider the following strategies:

- Spread your investments across asset classes: This reduces the risk that poor performance in one area will drag down your entire portfolio.
- Diversify within asset classes: Don't just invest in one stock or bond. Consider a range of sectors, industries, and

geographies.

- Adjust over time: As you approach retirement, you might want to shift towards more conservative investments to protect what you've accumulated.

Monitoring and rebalancing

Regularly checking in on your portfolio is vital. Over time, some investments may grow faster than others, skewing your original asset allocation. Here's how to keep your portfolio in line with your goals:

- Review your portfolio at least annually: This will help you determine whether your investments are still aligned with your retirement objectives.
- Rebalance when necessary: If your asset allocation drifts from your target, sell off some overperforming assets and buy more underperforming ones to get back on track.

Visual Element: Infographics on Portfolio Diversification

An infographic could visually break down the components of a diversified portfolio, showing examples of asset classes and how they might be combined based on different risk tolerances.

Interactive Element: Portfolio Builder Exercise

This is an online exercise where you input your retirement goals, risk tolerance, and investment preferences to receive suggestions for building a diversified portfolio. This tool can offer immediate, personalized insights into how diversification can work for you.

Textual Element: Real-life Diversification Strategies

This section offers insights from financial experts on diversifying investments. It can include quotes and advice on building a portfolio that withstands market volatility. It might cover topics like the importance of international investments or how emerging technologies create new investment opportunities.

By understanding and applying the principles of diversification, you're not just protecting your investments from the unpredictable nature of markets but also positioning yourself to take advantage of a range of opportunities. Like a well-curated art gallery, your portfolio should be a reflection of diverse and strategic choices that come together to create a cohesive and resilient financial future.

5.2 UNDERSTANDING RISK TOLERANCE AND TIME HORIZON

Defining Risk Tolerance

Risk tolerance is an investor's capacity to endure market volatility and the possibility of losing money on investments in the short term. It is a fundamental aspect that influences not just the selection of investments but also the ability to maintain a calm demeanor during market downturns. Individuals have varying levels of comfort with risk, shaped by their financial situation, investment experience, and even psychological disposition towards loss. Recognizing and accepting your risk tolerance is pivotal in creating an investment strategy you can stick with, avoiding panic-driven decisions during market fluctuations.

Assessing Your Risk Tolerance

Determining your personal risk tolerance involves introspection and, sometimes, complex evaluations. Here are steps to guide you through this essential process:

- Financial assessment: Examine your financial situation, including emergency funds, debts, and income stability. A solid monetary base can offer the leeway to take on more risk.
- Experience and knowledge: Reflect on your investment experience and understanding of financial markets. Familiarity can sometimes mitigate discomfort with volatility.
- Psychological comfort: Consider how you've reacted to past market downturns. Did you lose sleep over temporary losses, or could you see beyond the volatility toward long-term gains?
- Use tools and quizzes: Numerous online assessments can provide a rough estimate of your risk tolerance, combining various factors into a comprehensive analysis. While not definitive, these tools can offer a starting point for understanding your disposition toward investment risk.

Matching Investments to Your Risk Tolerance

Once you've gauged your risk tolerance, the next step is aligning your investment choices accordingly. This ensures your portfolio matches your comfort level, preventing rash decisions during market lows. Here's how to approach this alignment:

- Conservative investors might choose bonds, fixed-income funds, and high-quality dividend-paying stocks. These options offer stability and regular income, which is suitable for those with low-risk tolerance.
- Moderate investors could consider a balanced mix of stocks and bonds, providing a blend of growth potential and income. This middle ground suits those comfortable with some level of volatility but cautious of significant risks.
- Aggressive investors, comfortable with high volatility for the chance of higher returns, might focus on stocks, particularly

in high-growth sectors, or explore options like venture capital for part of their portfolio. Their higher risk tolerance allows them to weather market swings in pursuit of substantial gains.

Adjusting for Changes in Risk Tolerance

Risk tolerance is not static; it can evolve due to changes in your financial situation, nearing retirement, or shifts in market conditions. Hence, adjusting your investment strategy over time is crucial. Here are considerations for making these adjustments:

- Regular reviews: Periodically reassess your risk tolerance, especially after major life events such as marriage, the birth of a child, or receiving an inheritance. These changes can impact your financial goals and, by extension, how much risk you're willing to take.
- Gradual shifts in asset allocation: As you approach retirement, gradually reducing exposure to high-risk investments can help protect your savings. This doesn't mean a sudden switch but a thoughtful reallocation over time.
- Stay informed: Keeping abreast of financial news and market trends can help you make informed decisions about adjusting your portfolio in response to changing economic landscapes.

You can create a resilient strategy that supports your financial goals through careful assessment and alignment of your investments with your risk tolerance, coupled with adjustments as your situation and the markets change. This approach allows for a smoother investment experience tailored to your unique profile and life journey.

5.3 INDEX FUNDS AND ETFS: INVESTING MADE SIMPLE

Two investment vehicles stand out in retirement savings for their simplicity and effectiveness: index funds and exchange-traded funds (ETFs). These options provide a straightforward path for individuals looking to grow their retirement savings without becoming stock market experts. The allure of these investment types lies in their ability to offer broad market exposure, which is critical for building a resilient retirement portfolio.

Benefits of Index Funds and ETFs

Index funds and ETFs have gained popularity among investors for several reasons, paramount among them being their ability to mirror the performance of a market index. This could be a broad market index like the S&P 500 or a more specialized one focusing on a particular sector or region. This mirroring effect ensures that investors can participate in the collective performance of many companies, spreading out their risk and potential for returns. Another advantage is the transparency these funds offer, as their holdings reflect those of the indexes they track, allowing investors to know exactly where their money is at all times.

Cost-effectiveness

One of the most compelling arguments for choosing index funds and ETFs is their cost-effectiveness. These funds typically have lower management fees than actively managed funds because they follow a passive investment strategy. This means they do not require a team of analysts and portfolio managers to pick stocks, which can significantly reduce expenses. Lower fees mean more of your investment goes towards growing your retirement savings rather than covering administrative costs. Additionally, the tax efficiency of these funds, particularly ETFs, which often have lower capital gains distributions, can further enhance their attractiveness to investors focused on maximizing their retirement savings.

Selecting the Right Funds

With many options available, selecting suitable index funds and ETFs for your retirement portfolio can seem daunting. However, a few key considerations can guide your selection process:

- Match your risk tolerance and investment goals: Choose funds that align with your comfort with risk and long-term objectives. Consider bond index funds for a more conservative approach; for growth, look towards stock index funds.
- Consider the expense ratio: While these funds are known for cost-effectiveness, some still have higher fees than others. Opt for funds with a low expense ratio to maximize your investment returns.
- Diversification: Ensure the funds you select offer the diversification needed to protect your portfolio from volatility. This might mean choosing a mix of stock and bond funds and considering funds that provide exposure to international markets.

Passive vs. Active Management

The debate between passive and active management is central to investing in index funds and ETFs. Passive management, the strategy behind these funds, is predicated on the belief that it is difficult, if not impossible, for fund managers to consistently outperform the market over the long term. Therefore, passive funds can capture the market's returns by following a market index. This approach contrasts with active management, where fund managers attempt to beat the market through stock selection and timing. However, the higher fees associated with active management and the inconsistency in outperforming the market make passive index funds and ETFs a more attractive option for many retirement savers. Their simplicity, the potential for solid returns, and low costs make them essential to a retirement investment strategy.

In closing, index funds and ETFs represent a streamlined path to achieving a diversified and robust retirement portfolio. Their broad market exposure, combined with low costs and the efficiency of passive management, positions them as wise choices for investors aiming to grow their retirement savings. These investment vehicles demystify the retirement savings process, making it accessible to all, regardless of financial acumen. As we move forward, remember that the key to a successful retirement strategy lies in making informed choices that align with your goals, risk tolerance, and the changing landscape of the financial markets.

6

TAX-SAVVY STRATEGIES FOR RETIREMENT SAVINGS

I magine you've found an old map leading to hidden treasure. The map is complex, filled with symbols and paths. Navigating the tax implications of retirement savings can feel just as intricate, yet mastering this map can lead to substantial rewards—maximizing your wealth and minimizing your tax liabilities. This chapter is your guide, helping you decode the symbols and choose the best paths to ensure your retirement savings work as efficiently as possible, keeping more money in your pocket.

Tax Advantages of Retirement Accounts

Let's start with the basics. Different retirement accounts offer unique tax advantages that, when used strategically, can significantly enhance your savings. For instance, traditional IRAs and 401(k)s provide tax deductions on contributions, lowering your taxable income for the year you contribute. On the flip side, Roth IRAs and Roth 401(k)s, funded with after-tax dollars, promise tax-free withdrawals in retirement.

Consider this when planning contributions:

- If you're currently in a high tax bracket and expect to be in a lower one in retirement, traditional accounts might be more beneficial due to the immediate tax break.
- Conversely, if you're in a lower tax bracket now but expect to be in a higher one upon retirement, Roth accounts could save you on taxes in the long run.

Withdrawal Strategies to Minimize Taxes

When it comes time to withdraw your savings, having a smart strategy is crucial. Withdrawing from different types of accounts in a specific order can keep you in a lower tax bracket, reducing the tax impact.

- Start with withdrawals from your taxable accounts, such as brokerage accounts, as these can have a lower tax rate, especially if you're selling assets that qualify for long-term capital gains.
- Next, turn to your tax-deferred accounts like traditional IRAs and 401(k)s. Since these withdrawals are taxed as regular income, timing them to keep you within favorable tax brackets can be a game-changer.
- Save your Roth IRA and Roth 401(k) withdrawals for last. Since these are tax-free, they won't bump you into a higher tax bracket.

Understanding Tax Brackets

Getting a grip on how tax brackets work is like having a decoder ring for your financial map. In the U.S., the tax system is progressive, meaning the rate increases as your income does. Planning your retirement withdrawals to stay within the lower brackets can save you a significant amount in taxes.

- Monitor how your retirement accounts' required minimum distributions (RMDs) might impact your taxable income. Starting at age 72, these mandatory withdrawals could push you into a higher bracket if not carefully managed.
- Consider consolidating smaller accounts to simplify your RMDs and potentially keep you in a lower tax bracket.

Tax Implications of Social Security and Other Income

Social Security benefits can also play a role in your tax situation. Depending on your overall income, some of your benefits may be taxable. Here's what to keep in mind:

- If Social Security is your only source of income, your benefits likely won't be taxed.
- However, if you have other substantial income, up to 85% of your Social Security benefits could be subject to tax.
- Strategies like Roth conversions or tapping into your Roth accounts can help manage this, potentially reducing the tax on your Social Security benefits.

Visual Element: "Your Retirement Tax Map"

An infographic titled "Your Retirement Tax Map" could visually depict:

- The different retirement accounts and their tax treatments
- A suggested order of withdrawals to minimize taxes
- How tax brackets work and tips for staying in lower brackets

Interactive Element: "Tax Impact Calculator"

An online calculator where you input details about your retirement accounts, expected income, and age to see:

- How different withdrawal strategies could impact your taxes
- A visualization of potential tax savings over time

Textual Element: Real-life Tax Planning Strategies

A section dedicated to strategies people have used to navigate the tax landscape in retirement effectively, including:

- How timing withdrawals from various accounts helped them stay in a lower tax bracket.
- The impact of Roth conversions during lower-income years to minimize taxes long-term.

Navigating the tax implications of retirement savings can be manageable. With the proper knowledge and strategies, you can make informed decisions that protect your hard-earned savings from unnecessary taxes. This chapter has laid out the basics, giving you the tools to plot your course. As you move forward, remember that staying informed, flexible, and proactive in your tax planning can make all the difference in securing the retirement you envision.

6.1 ROTH CONVERSIONS: TIMING AND STRATEGY

A Roth conversion is a strategic move that involves transferring funds from a traditional IRA or 401(k) into a Roth IRA. This financial maneuver can be an advantageous part of your tax planning arsenal, especially if you anticipate being in a higher tax bracket in retirement than you are currently. Understanding when and how to execute a Roth conversion can significantly optimize your retirement savings and tax situation.

What is a Roth Conversion?

In essence, a Roth conversion shifts your savings from a tax-deferred account, where taxes are paid upon withdrawal, to a Roth account, which allows for tax-free growth and withdrawals in retirement. This process requires paying taxes on the converted amount in the year of the conversion. While the upfront tax bill may seem daunting, the long-term benefits of tax-free growth can outweigh the initial cost for many investors. This strategy is particularly appealing if you expect your tax rate to increase in the future, as it locks in the current lower tax rate on the converted funds.

Analyzing the Timing for a Roth Conversion

Timing is everything when it comes to a Roth conversion. The goal is to convert when it will result in the lowest tax burden, both now and in the future. Factors to consider include:

- Current and future tax rates: If you believe your tax rate will be higher in retirement, converting at today's lower rate can result in significant tax savings.
- Market conditions: A market downturn can be an opportune time to convert, as the reduced value of your investments will result in a lower tax bill on the conversion.
- Income fluctuations: Periods of lower income, such as a gap year between jobs, can also be an ideal time to convert since your overall tax rate may be lower.

Calculating the Cost and Benefits

A meticulous calculation is vital to weigh the pros and cons of a Roth conversion. Start by estimating the tax due on the amount you plan to convert, considering your current tax bracket and state taxes, if applicable. Next, project the potential growth of these funds in a Roth IRA, factoring in tax-free withdrawals in retirement. Compare this to the projected growth in a traditional IRA, considering future tax liabilities. Tools and calculators available online can assist in these projections, but consulting with a financial advisor for a personalized analysis is recommended.

Considerations include:

- Immediate tax implications: The added income from the conversion could push you into a higher tax bracket.
- Long-term tax savings: Compare the value of tax-free withdrawals from a Roth IRA against the deferred tax benefits of a traditional IRA.
- Required Minimum Distributions (RMDs): Traditional IRAs require RMDs starting at age 72, which can increase your taxable income in retirement. Roth IRAs do not have RMDs, potentially offering a more flexible retirement income strategy.

Case Studies

To illustrate the impact of Roth conversions, let's examine two scenarios:

- Case Study 1: Early Career Conversion John, in his early 30s, expects his income to grow significantly throughout his career. He converts $50,000 from his traditional IRA to a Roth IRA during a year when his income is lower due to a sabbatical. Despite the upfront tax payment, the conversion allows his investment to grow tax-free for over 30 years. By retirement, the tax-free withdrawals from his Roth IRA significantly outweigh the initial tax cost of the conversion.
- Case Study 2: Pre-Retirement Conversion Linda, in her late 50s, plans to retire in a high-tax state and expects her tax rate to increase. She strategically converts portions of her 401(k) to a Roth IRA over several years, staying within her current

lower tax bracket. This staggered approach minimizes her tax liability and sets her up for tax-free income in retirement, aligning perfectly with her financial goals.

These examples underscore the importance of strategic planning when considering a Roth conversion. The right timing and circumstances can lead to substantial tax savings and a more flexible retirement income strategy. However, every investor's situation is unique, and the decision to convert should be made with a thorough understanding of the potential costs and benefits.

6.2 HARVESTING TAX LOSSES TO OPTIMIZE RETIREMENT INCOME

Tax loss harvesting stands out for its elegance and effectiveness in the tapestry of seasoned investors' financial strategies to optimize their retirement income. While less familiar to some, this strategy is a powerful tool in the savvy investor's kit, offering a way to mitigate the impact of taxes on investment returns. Here, we explore the nuances of tax loss harvesting, from its basic definition to the strategies, limits, and integration into broader tax planning efforts to enhance retirement income.

Introduction to Tax Loss Harvesting

Tax loss harvesting involves selling investments that have declined in value to realize losses, which can be used to offset taxes on both gains and income. The idea is to turn the lemons of investment losses into the lemonade of tax reduction. It's a proactive approach that requires monitoring your portfolio for opportunities to realize losses without derailing your long-term investment goals.

Strategies for Effective Tax Loss Harvesting

Implementing tax loss harvesting within your retirement portfolio requires both timing and strategy. Here are some actionable steps:

- Regular Portfolio Review: Keep an eye on the performance of your investments, looking for positions that have lost value and might be candidates for selling.
- Matching Losses with Gains: If you have realized gains, look for losses that can offset these gains. This balancing act can effectively reduce your capital gains tax.
- Beware of the Wash Sale Rule: The IRS prohibits claiming a tax deduction for a security sold in a wash sale. This rule prevents investors from selling a security at a loss and repurchasing the same or substantially identical security within 30 days before or after the sale. To comply, consider replacing the sold asset with a different investment that meets your portfolio's diversification and asset allocation needs.
- Consider the Timing: While tax loss harvesting can be done anytime during the year, many investors look to implement this strategy towards the end of the year to offset realized capital gains. However, being too focused on a specific time can lead to missed opportunities or rushed decisions. Flexibility and attention throughout the year can yield better results.

Limits and Rules

The IRS has set clear guidelines and limits for tax loss harvesting to ensure compliance:

- $3,000 Limit: Investors can use capital losses to offset a maximum of $3,000 ($1,500 if married filing separately) of other income, such as wages or salaries, annually. Any excess losses can be carried forward to future years.

- Long-term vs. Short-term: The IRS distinguishes between long-term and short-term capital gains and losses. Short-term losses must offset short-term gains, and long-term losses must offset long-term gains. If additional losses remain, they can be applied to the opposite type of gain.

Integrating Tax Loss Harvesting with Overall Tax Planning

For those navigating the complexities of retirement income planning, integrating tax loss harvesting into your broader tax strategy can create a more cohesive approach to managing your finances. This integration involves several considerations:

- Holistic View: Look at your financial picture through a wide lens, considering all sources of income, including retirement accounts, Social Security benefits, and any part-time work, and how tax loss harvesting fits into this mix.
- Coordination with Financial Advisors: Work closely with your financial advisor or tax professional to ensure that tax loss harvesting aligns with your financial goals and tax planning strategies. This collaboration is critical to making informed decisions that benefit your financial well-being.
- Flexibility and Adaptation: The financial landscape and tax laws are ever-changing. It is crucial to stay informed and ready to adapt your strategies in response to new information and changes in your life circumstances.

Tax loss harvesting is more than just a tactical move in investment management; it reflects a thoughtful and adaptive approach to building your financial future. By acknowledging the inevitability of market fluctuations and positioning yourself to navigate these with an eye toward tax efficiency, you set the stage for a retirement income strategy that reflects both wisdom and foresight.

In closing, the journey through tax loss harvesting reveals it as a nuanced strategy that, when executed with care, enhances the fabric of your retirement savings plan. It underscores the importance of vigilance, strategic action, and the integration of investment decisions within the broader context of your financial life. As we move forward, the insights gleaned from this exploration of tax loss harvesting serve as a valuable companion, guiding you toward a future where your retirement savings are preserved and optimized for the long road ahead.

7

NAVIGATING HEALTHCARE COSTS IN RETIREMENT

I magine for a moment you're planning a cross-country road trip. Your route is mapped out, the car's tank is full, and you're ready to hit the road. But have you considered the pit stops for fuel, the occasional roadside diner for meals, or even potential detours due to unforeseen roadblocks? Much like this journey, planning for healthcare costs in retirement involves anticipating not just the predictable expenses but also preparing for the unexpected ones that might arise.

Healthcare is a critical aspect of retirement planning, often underestimated in its complexity and impact on retirement savings. Understanding how to project your healthcare needs, the role of Medicare, considerations for long-term care, and creating a healthcare budget are pivotal. Together, these elements shape a strategy that safeguards your retirement savings against potentially high healthcare costs.

Projecting Your Healthcare Needs

Estimating future healthcare needs involves examining your current health status, lifestyle, and family medical history. While it's impossible to predict every medical issue you might encounter, a realistic appraisal of these factors can offer valuable insights into potential healthcare needs and costs. For instance, if chronic conditions such as diabetes or heart disease run in your family, you might face similar issues, which could significantly impact your healthcare budget.

Here are steps to project your healthcare needs more accurately:

- Document your current health status: Track any existing conditions, medications, and regular healthcare services you use.
- Review your family medical history: This can give clues about what conditions you might be predisposed to.
- Consult healthcare providers: They can offer professional insights into how your current health might evolve and impact your future healthcare needs.

The Role of Medicare

Medicare is central to retirement healthcare planning but doesn't cover everything. Understanding what Medicare covers and what you'll need to budget for out-of-pocket is crucial. Generally, Medicare covers a portion of hospital stays, doctor visits, and some preventive services. However, it doesn't cover long-term care, most dental care, eye exams related to prescribing glasses, or hearing aids.

To navigate Medicare effectively:

- Educate yourself on the different parts of Medicare: Part A covers hospital insurance, Part B covers medical insurance, Part D covers prescription drugs, and Medicare Advantage Plans (Part C) offer an alternative way to receive your Medicare benefits.
- Consider a Medicare Supplement Insurance (Medigap) policy: This can help pay some of the healthcare costs that Original

Medicare doesn't cover, like copayments, coinsurance, and deductibles.

Long-Term Care Considerations

Long-term care could become necessary if you're unable to perform basic self-care tasks due to aging or illness. The cost of long-term care, whether provided at home or in a facility, can be substantial and is not covered by Medicare. Planning for this possibility is critical to a comprehensive retirement healthcare strategy.

Effective long-term care planning might involve:

- Researching long-term care insurance: While premiums can be high, especially if you purchase a policy later in life, the benefits can significantly offset the cost of long-term care services.
- Exploring other funding options: Depending on your financial situation, these might include savings, retirement income, or even reverse mortgages.

Creating a Healthcare Budget

A healthcare budget for retirement should account for premiums, out-of-pocket costs, and potential long-term care expenses. This budget is not static; it should be reviewed and adjusted as you age and as healthcare costs evolve.

Steps to create a healthcare budget include:

- Estimating annual healthcare expenses: Include Medicare premiums, out-of-pocket costs for services and medications not covered by Medicare, and Medigap premiums if applicable.
- Planning for inflation: Healthcare costs historically rise faster than general inflation, so it's wise to factor in higher costs

yearly.

- Considering long-term care costs: Even if you're healthy now, including long-term care costs in your budget ensures you're prepared for any eventuality.

Visual Element: Healthcare Costs Infographic

An infographic titled "Breaking Down Retirement Healthcare Costs" could visually represent:

- The average costs associated with Medicare premiums and out-of-pocket expenses.
- The percentage of retirees likely to need long-term care and the average cost of care.
- A pie chart showing the typical distribution of healthcare expenses in retirement.

Interactive Element: Healthcare Budget Calculator

An online calculator that allows you to input details such as current age, health status, and lifestyle factors could generate an estimated healthcare budget for retirement. This tool can help you visualize potential costs and adjust your retirement planning accordingly.

Healthcare planning in retirement is about more than just understanding Medicare; it's about anticipating your needs, knowing your options, and creating a budget that ensures your retirement savings can support your lifestyle and well-being. Like making those necessary pit stops on a long road trip, addressing healthcare costs in retirement ensures you can enjoy the journey without unexpected financial detours.

7.1 NAVIGATING MEDICARE: WHAT YOU NEED TO KNOW

Medicare is a cornerstone for retirees' healthcare in the United States, yet its various components can seem like a maze. A clear understanding of what Medicare entails and how its parts differ is necessary to make informed decisions. Knowing when to enroll and how to choose between additional coverage options can also significantly influence your healthcare experience and expenses in retirement.

Medicare Basics

Medicare is divided into distinct sections, each designed to cover different aspects of healthcare:

- Part A covers hospital stays, skilled nursing facility care, hospice, and home health care services. For most people, Part A comes without a monthly premium if they or their spouse paid Medicare taxes while working.
- Part B pays for doctor visits, outpatient care, medical supplies, and preventive services. Unlike Part A, Part B requires a monthly premium that varies based on your income.
- Part C, also known as Medicare Advantage, is an alternative to Original Medicare offered by private companies approved by Medicare. These plans include all benefits and services covered under Parts A and B, often providing additional coverage like vision, hearing, and dental.
- Part D adds prescription drug coverage to Original Medicare, some Medicare Cost Plans, some Medicare Private-Fee-for-Service Plans, and Medicare Medical Savings Account Plans. These plans are offered by insurance companies and other private companies approved by Medicare.

Understanding these parts is the first step in navigating Medicare effectively. Each plays a role in covering the spectrum of healthcare services you might need, yet they operate under different rules and costs.

Enrollment Timelines and Penalties

Timing is crucial when enrolling in Medicare. To sign up, you have a 7-month Initial Enrollment Period around your 65th birthday—3 months before, the month of, and 3 months after. Missing this window can lead to lifetime penalties and a gap in your healthcare coverage. For example, if you delay Part B enrollment, your monthly premium may go up 10% for each full 12-month period you were eligible but didn't enroll.

Special Enrollment Periods allow you to sign up for Part A and/or Part B during certain life events, like losing job-based coverage, without facing late penalties. Understanding these timelines ensures you avoid unnecessary costs and maintain continuous coverage.

Medigap and Medicare Advantage Plans

Deciding between Medigap and Medicare Advantage requires weighing their benefits against your healthcare needs and budget.

- Medigap policies supplement Original Medicare benefits by covering costs like deductibles, copayments, and coinsurance. These policies are standardized across most states, offering predictable coverage but not services like dental or vision. You cannot have both a Medigap policy and Medicare Advantage; it's one or the other.
- Medicare Advantage Plans bundle Medicare Parts A and B, and usually D, into one plan. They often include benefits not covered by Original Medicare, such as dental, vision, and hearing, sometimes at no extra cost. However, they come with network restrictions, meaning you may have to see providers within the plan's network for care.

Your choice impacts your out-of-pocket costs, and where you can receive care, so it's important to consider your health needs and preferences when making a decision.

Managing Costs with Medicare

Strategies to keep your healthcare expenses manageable with Medicare include:

- Review your coverage annually during the Open Enrollment Period. This is your chance to switch plans if you find another that better meets your needs or offers a better value.
- Understand your plan's out-of-pocket costs, including deductibles, copayments, and coinsurance. This knowledge helps budget for healthcare expenses throughout the year.
- If you take prescription drugs, consider a Part D plan. Review the plan's formulary to ensure it covers your medications and compare costs across plans.
- Use preventive services that Medicare covers, like flu shots and screening tests. These can help catch health issues early when they're more manageable and less costly.

Navigating Medicare effectively means staying informed about your options and how they align with your healthcare needs. By understanding its components, enrollment rules, and how to manage costs, you can make choices that support your health and financial well-being in retirement.

7.2 LONG-TERM CARE INSURANCE: IS IT RIGHT FOR YOU?

When considering the later stages of life, it's natural to consider the support you might need. Long-term care insurance emerges as a beacon for those who wish to prepare for the possibility of requiring extended medical or personal assistance. This form of insurance is designed to cover services not typically included in regular health insurance, Medicare, or Medicaid, such as in-home care, nursing home stays, or assisted living facilities.

The initial step involves a clear-eyed evaluation of what long-term care insurance entails. It's a policy you purchase to provide for the cost of long-term care beyond a predetermined period. Unlike traditional health insurance, it covers the cost of help with daily activities, like bathing and dressing, when you have a chronic medical condition, a disability, or a disorder such as Alzheimer's disease.

Evaluating the Need for Long-Term Care Insurance

Understanding your risk and the financial implications is crucial. Consider these factors:

- Personal and family health history can provide clues about your future needs. Genetics play a role in many conditions that require long-term care.
- Age and current health status: The younger and healthier you are when you buy the policy, the lower your premiums will be. However, buying too early could mean paying premiums for a more extended period.
- Financial resources: Assess whether you have the financial means to pay for care without insurance. Long-term care costs can quickly deplete savings, impacting the quality of life and inheritance of heirs.

Choosing the Right Policy

Not all long-term care insurance policies are created equal. When shopping for a policy, pay attention to these details:

- Coverage options: Policies can differ greatly in what they cover. Look for one that provides the flexibility to use your benefits in various settings, including your home, community organizations, or specialized facilities.

- Benefit period: The length of time a policy will pay out benefits can vary. Some may offer a few years of coverage, while others cover you for life.
- Elimination period: This refers to the time between when an injury or illness begins and when you start receiving benefits. Shorter elimination periods mean higher premiums.
- Inflation protection: With the cost of care rising, this feature adjusts your benefits over time to keep pace with inflation.

Alternatives to Traditional Long-Term Care Insurance

For those unsure about traditional long-term care insurance, alternatives exist:

- Hybrid insurance policies: These combine life insurance with long-term care coverage. You can access some of the death benefit early for long-term care, with the remainder paid out as a death benefit.
- Self-insurance: This strategy involves setting aside funds specifically for long-term care. It requires discipline and a solid investment plan but offers flexibility.
- Government programs: While Medicare's coverage is limited, Medicaid may provide for long-term care, primarily for those with low income and few assets.

Choosing the best way to plan for long-term care is a deeply personal decision. It hinges on your health outlook, financial situation, and individual preferences regarding the care you envision receiving. Taking the time to understand the nuances of long-term care insurance and its alternatives allows you to make an informed choice, one that aligns with your aspirations for your later years.

As we wrap up this exploration of long-term care insurance, remember that planning for the future extends beyond mere financial calculations. It's about ensuring peace of mind for yourself and your loved ones, knowing that you've taken steps to maintain your dignity and independence in later life. This thoughtful approach to planning illuminates the path forward, guiding you toward decisions that resonate with your values and long-term aspirations. With a clear strategy for managing healthcare costs, including the potential need for long-term care, you can confidently face the future.

As we transition from focusing on healthcare and long-term care planning, the next chapter shifts our attention to another vital aspect of retirement planning: ensuring your estate is in order. This progression from safeguarding your health to securing your legacy is a natural step in crafting a comprehensive retirement plan that reflects your desires for a vibrant retirement and your wishes for the impact you'll leave behind.

LET OTHERS KNOW THAT THE PERFECT TIME IS NOW

"Retirement is wonderful if you have two essentials—much to live on and much to live for."

— ANONYMOUS

Two of the most common reasons why people don't plan adequately for retirement have to do with time. For adults in their 30s or so, it may seem "too soon" to think about retirement. By contrast, those in their 50s and beyond who are struggling with saving as much as they'd like to or sorting through a complex financial mess may feel like it's "too late" to get back on track. My aim throughout this book has been to knock down these obstacles in one fell swoop. The decisions you make now—irrespective of your age or how close you are to retirement—have an enormous impact on your financial, physical, and mental health well-being, so if there is any topic that merits the cheer "Carpe Diem," it is most definitely retirement planning.

By this stage of your reading, you have already seen how smart retirement starts by taking a thorough, honest look at your current state of affairs. Next, it involves weighing the pros and cons of 401Ks and IRAs and deciding which aligns more closely with your current situation, assets, and life plan. You have seen that there are catch-up plans that are specifically catered for those who may have left planning to later stages of their career. I have also shared tools like the compounding calculator to help you gauge how much your savings can grow if you embrace the right strategies.

If you are already taking proactive steps toward a brighter financial future, I hope you can help someone who is struggling with retirement planning.

By leaving a review on Amazon, you'll show other readers where they can find a complete guide that will take them from the early stages of planning right through to passive wealth creation.

Thanks so much for your help. Financial literacy may be the one area that millions of people wish they had had better guidance with. Your words will let them know that this handy guide will help them make up for lost time so they can build a happier future.

Scan the QR code below

8

MAXIMIZING YOUR SOCIAL SECURITY

P icture this: every paycheck you've earned over the years is a brick. Some bricks are bigger, some smaller, but together, they've built the foundation for your retirement in the form of Social Security benefits. Unlike the straightforward process of piecing together a physical structure brick by brick, understanding how these financial building blocks translate into Social Security benefits can feel like deciphering an intricate puzzle. This chapter aims to simplify that puzzle, turning confusion into clarity.

8.1 UNDERSTANDING YOUR SOCIAL SECURITY BENEFITS

How Benefits Are Calculated

Social Security benefits are not pulled from thin air; they're meticulously calculated based on your earnings history. The formula considers your highest 35 years of earnings, adjusting for inflation. The aim is to provide a benefit that reflects your career's earning pattern. It's like looking back at the tapestry of your working life, highlighting the years that contributed most to your financial well-being.

- Average Indexed Monthly Earnings (AIME): This is where your 35 highest-earning years come into play, adjusted for inflation.
- Primary Insurance Amount (PIA): This is the base figure used to determine your benefit at full retirement age (FRA), calculated from your AIME using a progressive formula designed to benefit lower-income workers proportionately more.

The Impact of Work History

Your paycheck's size and the length of your career significantly impact your Social Security benefits. If you have yet to hit 35 years of work, zeros get factored into the calculation, which can pull down your benefit amount. On the other hand, higher-earning years can replace lower-earning ones in the formula, potentially increasing your benefit. It's akin to upgrading the bricks in your foundation with more substantial, more valuable materials as your career progresses.

- Years of work: Less than 35 years means zeros are included in your calculation, reducing your benefit.
- Earnings Record: Higher recent earnings can replace lower earnings from earlier in your work history, potentially increasing your benefit.

Spousal and Survivor Benefits

Social Security doesn't just look after you; it extends its support to your spouse and potentially other family members. Spousal benefits allow your husband or wife to receive up to 50% of your benefit at FRA, depending on their own Social Security record. Survivor benefits go a step further, providing your spouse up to 100% of your benefit in the event of your passing. It's a way of ensuring that the financial structure you've built offers shelter not just to you but to your loved ones as well.

- Spousal benefits: Up to 50% of the worker's FRA benefit is reduced if the spouse takes it before their own FRA.
- Survivor benefits: Up to 100% of the deceased worker's benefit is available to the spouse at their FRA.

Benefit Statements and Estimates

Understanding what you're projected to receive from Social Security is crucial for planning your retirement finances. Thankfully, the Social Security Administration (SSA) sends annual statements (now primarily online) that lay out your estimated benefits at various ages. These statements also provide a detailed record of your earnings history, allowing you to ensure all your bricks are accounted for accurately.

- Online: Create a "my Social Security" account on the SSA's website to access your statement and keep track of your estimated benefits.
- Accuracy Check: Use your annual statement to verify your earnings history and ensure your future benefits are calculated correctly.

Visual Element: Infographic on Social Security Calculation

An infographic titled "Decoding Your Social Security Benefits" could visually break down:

- The formula for calculating AIME and PIA.
- A comparison of benefits for different career lengths.
- How spousal and survivor benefits are determined.

Interactive Element: Social Security Benefit Calculator

An online calculator provided by the SSA allows you to input your earnings information and project your future benefits based on various retirement ages. This tool demystifies the calculation process, offering personalized insights into how your work history translates into retirement income.

Textual Element: Navigating Spousal Benefits

A detailed guide on optimizing spousal benefits could cover the following:

- Strategies for couples to consider when claiming benefits to maximize their total income.
- Real-life scenarios where one spouse's work history significantly influences the couple's Social Security planning.
- Tips for ensuring your spouse is positioned to receive the maximum possible survivor benefits.

Understanding your Social Security benefits is akin to reading a map of your financial future. With the proper knowledge and tools, you can confidently navigate this landscape, making informed decisions that ensure your retirement is as robust and rewarding as the career that paved the way for it.

8.2 THE BEST TIME TO START TAKING SOCIAL SECURITY

Navigating when to begin claiming Social Security benefits involves weighing various factors, each with its financial implications. This strategic choice can significantly influence your retirement income and demands careful consideration.

Early vs. Full Retirement Age

The age at which you choose to start receiving Social Security benefits impacts the monthly amount you will receive. Opting to take benefits before reaching your full retirement age (FRA), which ranges from 66 to 67 depending on your birth year, reduces benefits. On the other hand, delaying benefits beyond your FRA can increase your monthly amount by a certain percentage until you reach 70.

- Early Claiming: Starting benefits between the ages of 62 and your FRA reduces your monthly benefit. This reduction is permanent and can range from a 25% to 30% decrease, depending on your FRA.
- At Full Retirement Age: Claiming at your FRA entitles you to your full benefit amount, calculated based on your lifetime earnings.
- Delaying Benefits: For each year you delay past your FRA, your benefit increases by about 8% until you reach 70. This increase creates an incentive to wait, but it's not the best choice for everyone.

Breakeven Analysis

A breakeven analysis can illuminate when the total value of starting benefits early equals the total value of waiting until later. This calculation considers your cumulative benefits over time, comparing different start ages.

- To perform this analysis, you'll need to estimate the monthly benefit amounts you'd receive at different claiming ages.
- Factor in how long you would need to receive the higher delayed benefits to compensate for the years you didn't receive benefits by waiting.

This analysis can help clarify how long it would take for the decision to delay benefits to financially "pay off," considering the foregone benefits in the earlier years.

Personal Factors Affecting Your Decision

Several personal considerations can influence the optimal time for you to start receiving Social Security:

- Health and Life Expectancy: If you're in good health and have a family history of longevity, delaying benefits could result in a higher lifetime income. Conversely, claiming earlier might make more sense if you have health concerns or a shorter life expectancy.
- Financial Needs: Immediate financial needs may necessitate claiming benefits earlier. If you can comfortably cover your expenses without Social Security, waiting for an increased benefit could be advantageous.
- Employment Status: Working while receiving benefits before your FRA can temporarily reduce your benefits if your earnings exceed certain limits. This might encourage some to delay claiming.

Strategies for Married Couples

Married couples have unique opportunities to optimize their combined Social Security benefits. Coordinating when and how you each claim benefits can maximize your lifetime income.

- Consider Both Lifespans: When one spouse has a significantly higher benefit, it may be beneficial for that spouse to delay claiming. This strategy ensures the surviving spouse receives the highest possible survivor benefit.
- Claim and Suspend: While recent rule changes have limited the effectiveness of some strategies, a version of "claim and

suspend" can still be beneficial in specific situations. For example, if the higher-earning spouse delays their benefit to increase it but the other spouse needs to claim their spousal benefit, navigating these rules effectively can optimize your combined benefits.

- Minimize Taxes: The timing of your claims can also impact your tax situation, especially if you have other sources of income. Coordinating your Social Security benefits with withdrawals from retirement accounts can help minimize your tax liability.

For married couples, these strategies underscore the importance of viewing your Social Security decisions as part of a broader financial plan that considers your individual and joint needs and goals.

In summary, the decision of when to start taking Social Security benefits is multifaceted, influenced by a range of personal and financial factors. Whether navigating this decision solo or with a spouse, understanding the implications of early versus delayed claiming, performing a breakeven analysis, and considering your unique circumstances can guide you to a choice that supports your financial security in retirement.

8.3 STRATEGIES FOR MARRIED COUPLES TO MAXIMIZE BENEFITS

Navigating Social Security can be notably more intricate for married couples, presenting both opportunities and challenges in optimizing benefits. A well-coordinated approach enhances household income and ensures financial stability for the surviving spouse. Here, we explore specific strategies couples may employ, mindful of the nuances that could influence their decisions.

File and Suspend Strategy

The file-and-suspend strategy was a popular method, allowing one spouse to claim benefits based on the other's record while the latter's benefits continued to grow. However, significant changes to Social Security rules in 2015 have largely phased out this option. Previously, a higher-earning spouse could file for benefits at full retirement age and immediately suspend them. This action allowed the lower-earning spouse to claim a spousal benefit while the higher earner's benefits accrued delayed retirement credits. Under current regulations, if you suspend your benefits, no benefits can be paid to others based on your record during the suspension. This change underscores the importance of staying current with Social Security regulations, as evolving rules can impact planning strategies.

Restricted Application Strategy

The restricted application strategy remains a viable option for some couples. This tactic permits one spouse who has reached full retirement age to claim only spousal benefits while deferring their own benefits to accumulate delayed retirement credits. It's key to note that this strategy is only available to individuals born before January 2, 1954. For those eligible, it offers a way to boost household income in retirement without compromising the growth of their retirement benefits. This approach requires careful timing and understanding of eligibility criteria to ensure it aligns with your broader retirement planning goals.

Coordinating Retirement and Benefits

Effectively coordinating retirement dates and Social Security claiming strategies can significantly impact a couple's financial landscape in retirement. Couples should consider various factors, including age differences, health status, and whether both spouses have similar earnings histories or if one has notably higher earnings.

For instance, in scenarios where one spouse has a much lower earnings record, it might make sense for the higher earner to delay claiming benefits to maximize the survivor benefit. Simultaneously, the lower earner could claim benefits earlier, providing additional income in the short term. This coordinated approach ensures a balanced income stream throughout retirement while safeguarding the financial security of the surviving spouse.

Impact of Divorce and Widowhood

Social Security benefits also extend protections to divorced spouses and widows or widowers, offering avenues for them to claim benefits based on their former spouse's earning record. Divorced individuals may qualify for benefits on their ex-spouse's record if the marriage lasted at least ten years. They must also remain unmarried and be at least 62 years old. Similarly, widows and widowers can receive survivor benefits as early as 60. Understanding these provisions is crucial for individuals navigating the complexities of divorce or widowhood, as these benefits can provide a critical source of income in the absence of their spouse's earnings.

In the intricate dance of planning for retirement, married couples possess several moves at their disposal to maximize their Social Security benefits. From considering the implications of recent rule changes to employing strategies like restricted application and thoughtful coordination of benefits, couples are equipped with tools to enhance their financial well-being in retirement. However, it's essential to approach these strategies with a clear understanding of the rules and an eye toward how they fit into your overall retirement plan. This careful planning and coordination ensure that both spouses, and eventually the surviving spouse, are supported by the most robust financial framework.

As we close this chapter on Social Security strategies for married couples, the key takeaways center on the importance of informed decision-making and strategic planning. These approaches optimize your benefits and secure a stable financial foundation for the years ahead. With a thorough grasp of your options and the implications of your choices, you're better positioned to navigate the complexities of retirement planning. Now, as we transition from the specifics of Social Security to exploring estate and legacy planning, we continue to build on the foundation laid here, focusing next on securing and managing your assets for the future.

9

ESTATE PLANNING MADE CLEAR

I magine a scenario where you've spent a lifetime gathering pieces to an intricate puzzle: your estate. When put together correctly, this puzzle represents a clear picture of your wishes for your assets and legacy. Now, consider the challenge of ensuring this puzzle gets solved precisely as you envisioned after you're gone. That's where estate planning steps in, acting as the blueprint for assembling the pieces in your absence. It's not simply about wealth distribution; it's about making heartfelt decisions today that affect your loved ones tomorrow.

Estate planning often brings to mind complex legal documents and difficult conversations, leading many to put it off indefinitely. However, breaking down the process into understandable components can turn a daunting task into a manageable one. This chapter aims to shed light on the basics of wills and trusts, guide you in choosing the right executor or trustee, explain the probate process, and highlight common mistakes to avoid, all to ensure your estate plan stands on a solid foundation.

The Basics of Wills and Trusts

A will is a legal document detailing how you want your assets distributed after death. It's like leaving behind detailed instructions for a trusted friend on how to care for your prized possessions. Meanwhile, trusts offer a way to manage your assets both during your lifetime and after, with the benefit of potentially avoiding the lengthy probate process. Think of a trust as a secure box where you can place your assets, which a chosen individual, the trustee, holds the key to for the benefit of your chosen beneficiaries.

Choosing between a will and a trust, or deciding to use both, depends on various factors, including the size of your estate, your privacy concerns, and your goals for asset distribution. While a will might suffice for straightforward estates, a trust can offer more control over when and how your assets are distributed.

Choosing an Executor or Trustee

Selecting the right person to manage your estate or trust is akin to choosing the captain of a ship who will navigate your financial legacy through potentially choppy waters. This role requires someone trustworthy and capable of handling financial matters and the intricacies of estate administration. Often, people choose a close family member because of their familiarity with the family dynamics. Still, it's also wise to consider their financial acumen and organizational skills. In some cases, appointing a professional, such as an attorney or a financial advisor, might be the best route to ensure your estate is managed according to your wishes.

The Probate Process

Probate is the legal process of reviewing a will to determine its authenticity and validity. It's often misunderstood and feared for its potential to be time-consuming and costly. However, understanding this process can demystify it and reveal strategies for simplification. For instance, assets held in a trust, designated as "payable on death" (POD) or "transfer on death" (TOD), and jointly held assets often bypass probate entirely. Many states offer an expedited probate process for smaller estates, reducing the time and paperwork required.

Common Mistakes to Avoid

In estate planning, even minor oversights can lead to significant issues. Some common pitfalls include:

- Failing to update your estate plan: Life changes such as marriage, divorce, and the birth of children should trigger a review and, if necessary, an update to your estate plan.
- Neglecting digital assets: In today's digital age, including digital assets like social media accounts and digital currencies in your estate plan is crucial.
- Overlooking the impact of taxes: Proper estate planning can help minimize the tax burden on your heirs, ensuring they receive the maximum benefit from their inheritance.

Visual Element: Estate Planning Checklist

A comprehensive checklist can visually guide readers through the estate planning process, ensuring no detail is overlooked. This checklist could cover everything from gathering important documents to considering tax implications, and it would serve as a handy reference for anyone embarking on estate planning.

Interactive Element: Executor/Trustee Decision Tool

An online tool could help individuals decide who might be the best fit to manage their estate or trust. Users could gain insights into the most suitable candidates by answering questions about their potential choices, such as financial savvy, organizational skills, and emotional resilience.

Estate planning is more than just a set of legal documents; it's a thoughtful process that ensures your legacy is preserved and your loved ones are cared for according to your wishes. With a clear understanding of the basics and a strategic approach to avoid common pitfalls, you can build a solid estate plan that stands the test of time.

9.1 ESTATE PLANNING TOOLS EVERYONE SHOULD CONSIDER

Estate planning encompasses a variety of tools beyond wills and trusts, each playing a unique role in ensuring your wishes are respected and your loved ones are protected. From designating someone to make decisions on your behalf to directing how specific assets should be distributed, these tools form the backbone of a solid estate plan.

Durable Powers of Attorney

A durable power of attorney is an indispensable instrument, granting someone you trust the authority to manage your financial affairs if you're unable to do so. This could be due to illness, injury, or any other incapacity. Unlike a standard power of attorney, which becomes invalid if you become incapacitated, the "durable" aspect remains in effect, ensuring continuity in managing your financial responsibilities. It's a preemptive measure, preventing potential legal battles or delays in decision-making that could adversely affect your estate and financial well-being.

When setting up a durable power of attorney, you'll select an agent, typically a trusted family member or friend, who will have the legal authority to handle tasks such as paying bills, managing investments, and even selling property on your behalf. It's a role that requires trust and responsibility, underscoring the importance of choosing someone who understands your preferences and can act in your best interests.

Advance Healthcare Directives

Advance healthcare directives, comprising living wills and healthcare powers of attorney, provide instructions on your healthcare preferences in situations where you're unable to communicate them yourself. A living will outlines the types of medical treatments and life-sustaining measures you do or do not want, such as mechanical ventilation or feeding tubes, in the event of a terminal illness or permanent unconsciousness.

A healthcare power of attorney, on the other hand, designates a representative to make healthcare decisions on your behalf, guided by the preferences you've outlined in your living will. This combination ensures that your healthcare wishes are known and respected. It provides peace of mind to you and your family by clarifying your desires in advance and designating a trusted person to advocate for them.

Beneficiary Designations and POD/TOD Accounts

Beneficiary designations on retirement accounts, life insurance policies, and other assets bypass the will and probate process, directly transferring the asset to the named beneficiary upon your death. This straightforward way ensures that specific assets are passed to the intended individuals without delay. Regularly reviewing and updating these designations is critical, especially after major life events like marriage, divorce, or the birth of a child, to ensure they reflect your current wishes.

Similarly, payable on death (POD) and transfer on death (TOD) accounts offer a simple mechanism to transfer assets like bank accounts and securities directly to a designated beneficiary without going through probate. Once you register an account as POD or TOD and name a beneficiary, the assets in the account will automatically transfer to the beneficiary upon your death, streamlining the distribution process and providing immediate access to funds that may be needed for expenses.

Life Insurance in Estate Planning

Life insurance is pivotal in estate planning, offering a versatile tool for meeting various estate planning goals. Beyond providing financial support to your beneficiaries, life insurance proceeds can be used to pay estate taxes, debts, and final expenses, ensuring your estate can be distributed as you intended without being diminished by outstanding obligations.

Strategically, life insurance can also be used to equalize inheritances among beneficiaries. If, for instance, you wish to leave a family business to one child, life insurance can provide equivalent value to your other children, maintaining balance and reducing potential conflicts.

For those with larger estates, life insurance can be structured to fund a trust, offering additional control over how the proceeds are used and distributed. This can be particularly useful in providing for minor children, dependents with special needs, or managing the distribution of assets over time according to the conditions you set.

Incorporating these estate planning tools into your overall plan provides a more straightforward path for managing your affairs. It offers reassurance that your wishes will be honored and your loved ones will be cared for. Each tool serves a specific purpose, from ensuring decisions can be made during times of incapacity to directing the distribution of your assets according to your wishes. Careful consideration and regular review of these instruments are vital to maintaining an estate plan that accurately reflects your desires and adapts to your changing life circumstances.

9.2 BENEFICIARY DESIGNATIONS: AVOIDING COMMON MISTAKES

The clarity of our intentions plays a pivotal role in crafting a secure future for our loved ones. Nowhere is this clearer than in the realm of beneficiary designations. These selections, often made in a moment and tucked away in the documents of various accounts, carry the weight of our wishes beyond our lifetime. Yet, the simplicity of making these designations belies the complexity of their impact, making it crucial to approach them with precision and foresight.

The Critical Role of Accurate Beneficiary Designations

The act of naming a beneficiary is, at its heart, an act of specifying the future stewards of our assets. Whether for a retirement account, life insurance policy, or investment portfolio, these designations direct the flow of our assets directly to the named individuals, bypassing the often lengthy and complex probate process. However, inaccuracies or oversights in these designations can lead to unintended consequences, diverting assets from those we intended to benefit, potentially sparking disputes among loved ones, or contributing to legal challenges. The accuracy of these designations is not merely a detail but a cornerstone of effective estate planning.

Regular Reviews and Updates: A Necessity

Life is a tapestry of change, with significant events weaving new patterns into the fabric of our experiences. Marriages, births, divorces, and deaths reshape our relationships and, by extension, our estate planning intentions. Therefore, it is essential to review our beneficiary designations periodically and, if necessary, update them to reflect our current wishes accurately. This process ensures that the individuals we intend to support are the ones who will ultimately benefit from our assets, aligning our estate planning documents with the evolving landscape of our lives.

Ensuring Alignment with Your Estate Plan

Beneficiary designations, while powerful, are only one piece of the broader estate planning puzzle. To ensure a harmonious picture, these designations must be meticulously coordinated with the other elements of your estate plan, including your will, trusts, and powers of attorney. This coordination ensures a seamless transition of assets, reflecting a unified vision rather than a fragmented array of disjointed instructions. For instance, if your will outlines a specific distribution of assets, but your beneficiary designations direct those assets elsewhere, the latter will prevail. Regular consultations with estate planning professionals can help navigate these complexities, ensuring that your beneficiary designations complement and reinforce your overall estate planning objectives.

Navigating Special Situations

Life's intricacies often present us with unique situations that require thoughtful consideration in our estate planning:

- Minors as Beneficiaries: Directly naming minors as beneficiaries can complicate the distribution of assets, as minors are legally unable to take control of the assets until they reach adulthood. Establishing a trust or using a custodial account under the Uniform Transfers to Minors Act (UTMA) or the Uniform Gifts to Minors Act (UGMA) allows for a more structured management and distribution of assets to minor beneficiaries.
- Complex Family Dynamics: In families with complicated relationships, clear and carefully considered beneficiary designations can help prevent conflicts and ensure that assets are distributed according to your wishes. In these cases, it is wise to be explicit about your intentions, including a letter of explanation with your estate planning documents to provide context for your decisions.

This section of our exploration underscores the nuanced nature of beneficiary designations within the broader scope of estate planning. By emphasizing accuracy, advocating for regular reviews, ensuring alignment with overall estate planning goals, and thoughtfully addressing special situations, we pave the way for our assets to support our loved ones according to our true intentions.

As we conclude this exploration of estate planning, it's evident that the decisions we make today, from the grand strategies to the minute details, shape the legacy we leave behind. Our journey through wills, trusts, powers of attorney, and beneficiary designations reveals a landscape where foresight, clarity, and regular review guide us toward our estate planning goals. With these principles in mind, we move forward, prepared to face the future with confidence, knowing that our plans are crafted not just for our peace of mind but for the benefit and well-being of those we cherish most.

10

CRAFTING A FULFILLING RETIREMENT

Retirement opens the door to a new phase of life, one abundant with time previously spoken for by the demands of a career. It's a period ripe with potential, waiting to be shaped into whatever form you desire. However, without the structure work often provides, you might find yourself at a loss for what to do next. This chapter is dedicated to filling that canvas with vibrant purpose, engagement, and personal growth.

10.1 FINDING PURPOSE AFTER RETIREMENT

Exploring New Interests

Imagine standing in front of a buffet filled with more dishes than you could possibly try in one sitting. Retirement is much the same, offering a plethora of activities and interests to explore. Now is the time to try your hand at painting, start that garden, or learn to play the piano—activities you might have put on the back burner. Local community centers and online platforms offer classes ranging from art to zoology. Pick something that piques your curiosity. Who knows? You might discover a passion you never knew you had.

Volunteering and Giving Back

Giving your time to causes you care about can be incredibly rewarding. It's a chance to give back to your community, connect with like-minded individuals, and make a tangible difference. Whether mentoring young students, working at a food bank, or participating in environmental clean-ups, volunteering offers a sense of purpose and fulfillment. Consider the causes close to your heart, and explore how you can contribute. Many non-profits and charities constantly need volunteers and would welcome your help.

Continued Learning Opportunities

The pursuit of knowledge doesn't have an expiration date. Retirement is an excellent opportunity to dive deeper into subjects that intrigue you or to explore entirely new fields. Many universities and colleges offer reduced or free tuition for seniors, and online courses provide flexibility to learn at your own pace from the comfort of your home. Whether it's taking a course in history, attending a workshop on digital photography, or joining a book club, continued learning keeps your mind sharp and engaged.

Setting New Goals

Retirement doesn't mean the end of achieving goals; rather, it marks the beginning of new ones. These goals might be personal, like improving your fitness level, or more outward-facing, like starting a blog to share your life experiences. Setting goals gives you something to work toward and can help structure your days. Ensure these goals are specific, measurable, achievable, relevant, and time-bound (SMART) to keep you motivated and on track.

Visual Element: "Retirement Bucket List"

An infographic showcases various activities, hobbies, and goals one might pursue in retirement. Categories could include travel, education, hobbies, volunteering, and personal development, each with inspiring icons or images.

Interactive Element: "What's Your Retirement Passion?" Quiz

An online quiz designed to help retirees discover new interests or hobbies based on their preferences and personality. Questions could range from preferred ways to spend a day to how they like to interact with others, culminating in personalized suggestions for activities to explore.

Textual Element: Real-life Examples of Post-retirement Projects

A collection of brief stories highlighting retirees who found fulfilling post-retirement projects or hobbies. This could include someone who took up beekeeping, another who started a community garden, or someone else who wrote and published their first novel. These real-life examples serve as inspiration and a testament to the limitless possibilities retirement holds.

Retirement is not just about leaving the workforce; it's about entering a stage of life where you have the freedom to design your days as you see fit. It's a time for exploration, contribution, learning, and personal growth. By exploring new interests, volunteering, pursuing continued learning opportunities, and setting new goals, you can craft a fulfilling and enriching retirement in every aspect.

10.2 STAYING ACTIVE AND CONNECTED IN RETIREMENT

A fulfilling retirement is not solely about managing your finances but also about maintaining your health, nurturing your social connections, and embracing life's adventures. This section delves into the importance of physical activity, the benefits of social engagement, the thrill of travel and adventure, and the joy of hobbies and clubs.

Physical Activity for Health

The significance of regular physical activity can't be overstated, especially as you transition into retirement. Regular exercise is crucial for sustaining your health, enhancing your mood, and increasing your energy levels. Activities like walking, cycling, swimming, or participating in group fitness classes keep your body in peak condition and provide opportunities for social interaction. Consider activities you enjoy and are likely to stick with, whether it's yoga, dance classes, or even joining a local hiking group. Remember, the goal is to find joy in movement, making it a part of your daily routine that you look forward to.

Social Engagement

Staying socially engaged as you transition into retirement is vital to your well-being. It's a time when you can nurture existing relationships and cultivate new ones. Here are a few strategies to ensure you remain connected:

- Reconnect with old friends: Retirement can provide you with the time needed to rekindle friendships that may have waned due to the busyness of career and family life.
- Family time: With more flexibility in your schedule, you can create deeper bonds with family members. Regular family gatherings can strengthen these ties, whether in person or via video calls.

- Community involvement: Engaging in community events or joining local clubs can expand your social circle and connect you with individuals who share similar interests.
- Social media and technology: Embracing social media platforms and communication technologies can help you stay in touch with friends and family members, regardless of distance.

Travel and Adventure

Retirement opens up a wealth of opportunities for travel and adventure, allowing you to explore new cultures, cuisines, and landscapes. Here are some tips for making the most of your travel experiences, even on a budget:

- Plan off-season trips: Traveling during off-peak times can significantly reduce costs and offer a more relaxed experience with fewer tourists.
- Home exchanges and rentals: Consider home exchange programs or renting apartments instead of staying in hotels. This can offer a more authentic and cost-effective experience.
- Group travel: Joining travel groups or clubs can provide companionship and often leads to discounts on trips planned for members.
- Local adventures: Don't overlook the adventures that await you closer to home. Exploring local parks, museums, and historical sites can satisfy your sense of adventure without the need for extensive travel.

Hobbies and Clubs

Diving into hobbies and joining clubs provide meaningful ways to spend time, learn new skills, and meet people. Here are some suggestions to get you started:

- Gardening clubs: If you have a green thumb, or even if you're a novice looking to learn, gardening clubs offer a great way to connect with nature and fellow gardening enthusiasts.
- Book clubs: For those who love reading, book clubs offer a structured way to explore different genres and provide a social setting to discuss ideas and opinions.
- Crafting and art classes: Local community centers often offer classes in various crafts and arts. These can be wonderful creative outlets and great places to form new friendships.
- Sports clubs: Joining a golf club, tennis club, or bowling league can keep you active while offering a competitive yet friendly social environment.

In embracing these activities and strategies for staying active and connected, retirement can be transformed into a period of life that's as enriching and fulfilling as any other. With physical health, social engagement, and the pursuit of interests at the forefront, the days ahead promise to be vibrant and purposeful.

10.3 BUDGETING FOR HOBBIES AND TRAVEL IN RETIREMENT

The golden years of retirement bring with them a wealth of time to explore, learn, and indulge in activities that bring joy and fulfillment. Yet, aligning these pursuits with a well-thought-out budget ensures that this period is rich in experiences and financially sustainable. Here's a roadmap to crafting a leisure budget that supports your dreams without compromising your financial health.

Creating a Leisure Budget

Initiating this process requires a clear view of your overall retirement finances. From the outset, delineate a portion of your budget dedicated solely to leisure—hobbies, travel, or other pursuits that enliven your days. This budget segment is your ticket to adventure, creativity, and discovery. Begin by listing your monthly or annual retirement income sources alongside your fixed and variable expenses. The residue, post the essentials, earmarks your potential leisure fund. Using tools like spreadsheets or budgeting apps can simplify tracking and adjusting this budget as you navigate through retirement.

Prioritizing Spending

With your leisure budget defined, the next step is prioritizing how these funds will be allocated. Not all hobbies or travel desires carry the same weight of importance or fulfillment. Sit down with a notepad or digital document and list your leisure interests in order of significance. Perhaps sailing the Mediterranean tops your list, followed by photography classes, then golf club memberships. This prioritization acts as a guide, ensuring funds flow first to what matters most, enhancing satisfaction from your leisure budget.

Cost-saving Tips

Stretching your leisure budget without sacrificing enjoyment is an art in itself. Here are some strategies to get the most out of every dollar:

- Leverage Discounts: Many organizations offer discounts for seniors. Museums, parks, educational institutions, and travel services often provide reduced rates that can make activities more accessible.
- Embrace Off-peak Travel: Airfare and accommodations often see a dip in prices during off-peak seasons. Planning trips during these times can save substantially, allowing for more or extended adventures.
- DIY Over Buying: Engaging in hobbies like gardening, crafting, or woodworking? Consider do-it-yourself projects over purchasing ready-made items. Not only does this save money, but it also adds a personal touch and a sense of achievement.

- Share Experiences: Group activities or travel can split costs among participants. Organize a painting group or a local exploration team, or travel with friends to share the financial load.

Investing in Experiences

The true value in allocating funds for hobbies and travel lies in the experiences and memories created rather than the material possessions acquired. Studies suggest that experiences contribute more significantly to long-term happiness than tangible items. When planning how to utilize your leisure budget, consider options that promise new learning, adventure, and the joy of discovery. Whether mastering a new skill, witnessing the aurora borealis, or immersing in a foreign culture, these experiences enrich your life tapestry in irreplaceable ways.

As this chapter on enriching your retirement through well-planned hobbies and travel concludes, remember that the essence of a fulfilling retirement lies in balancing financial wisdom with the pursuit of passions. This delicate equilibrium ensures that your retirement years are financially secure and brimming with joy, growth, and adventure. As we transition to the next chapter, we carry forward the principles of thoughtful planning and wise spending, applying them to the broader context of maintaining health and vitality in retirement.

11

NAVIGATING NEW WATERS: IDENTITY AND FINANCE IN RETIREMENT

The moment you step away from your work life, it's as if you've set sail from the familiar shores of your career into the vast, uncharted waters of retirement. For many, work provides more than just a paycheck; it offers a sense of purpose, a framework for daily life, and, importantly, a component of one's identity. The transition into retirement, therefore, isn't just about adjusting your financial sails; it's equally about steering through the emotional currents that come with redefining who you are beyond your profession.

11.1 COPING WITH THE IDENTITY SHIFT IN RETIREMENT

Adjusting to Life Without Work

Changing from a structured work life to the freedom of retirement can feel like switching from a fast-paced sprint to a leisurely stroll. Suddenly, the routines that governed your days are gone, and the professional title that may have formed a part of your identity is no longer applicable. Acknowledging this shift is the first step. Recognize that it's normal to feel a mix of relief and disorientation. Many find solace in gradually reducing work hours before fully retiring, offering a smoother transition.

Rediscovering Yourself

Retirement opens up a space for self-discovery. Think back to interests and passions you might have shelved due to work commitments. Was there a hobby you loved or perhaps an interest you never had the time to explore? Now's the chance to pursue these with vigor. Whether painting, gardening, or learning a new language, engaging in these activities can be immensely fulfilling and form part of your new identity.

Building a New Routine

Creating a new routine is vital for shaping your days. Without the external structure work provided, it might quickly feel untethered. Start by setting regular times for meals, exercise, and hobbies. Plan outings and social engagements in advance. This structure doesn't have to be rigid; the beauty of retirement is having the flexibility to adjust your schedule as you please. Yet, a semblance of routine can provide comfort and a sense of normalcy.

Seeking Support

Finding others who are navigating the same transition can be incredibly reassuring. Consider joining retirement groups or forums where you can share experiences and tips. Talking to a counselor can provide professional guidance if the identity shift feels particularly challenging. Remember, seeking support is a sign of strength, not weakness.

Visual Element: "The Retirement Identity Compass"

An infographic that visually represents the journey of rediscovering one's identity in retirement. It could feature four main directions: North for exploring new interests, South for building a new routine, East for seeking support, and West for adjusting to life without work. Each direction could offer tips and activities to guide retirees in navigating this transition.

Interactive Element: "Rediscover Your Passions" Quiz

An online quiz that prompts retirees to answer questions about their preferences, pastimes, and dreams. The outcome could suggest new hobbies or activities to explore, tailored to their interests. This interactive tool would be engaging and provide personalized suggestions to help retirees embark on a path of self-discovery.

Textual Element: Real-life Adjustments Checklist

A checklist includes practical steps for adjusting to retirement, covering how to phase out of work, ways to explore new interests, tips for building a new routine, and resources for finding support. This checklist could serve as a tangible guide for retirees, helping them to navigate the emotional aspects of this transition with confidence.

Adjusting to life without work involves more than just filling your days with activities; it's about redefining your sense of self outside of your career. Rediscovering your passions, establishing a new routine, and seeking support are all crucial steps in this journey. Remember, retirement isn't just an end to work; it's an opportunity to design a life that reflects your true self, unbound by job titles or workplace identities.

11.2 PROTECTING YOUR RETIREMENT SAVINGS FROM INFLATION

The value of money doesn't remain static. Over time, inflation can subtly erode its purchasing power, turning today's comfortable nest egg into tomorrow's scanty sum. For retirees, understanding and mitigating the risks associated with inflation is crucial for safeguarding the longevity of their savings.

Understanding Inflation Risks

Inflation represents the rate at which the general level of prices for goods and services rises, subsequently eroding purchasing power. For those in retirement, the impact is twofold. While living expenses climb, the value of their savings may not keep pace, potentially diminishing their standard of living. Recognizing this risk is the first step. The next involves devising strategies to shield your savings from inflation's grasp, ensuring your financial well-being remains intact throughout your retirement.

Investment Strategies for Inflation

To fortify your retirement savings against inflation, incorporating investment strategies designed to counteract its effects can be highly effective.

- Treasury Inflation-Protected Securities (TIPS): TIPS are government bonds indexed to inflation and designed to increase in value along with the Consumer Price Index. The principal value of TIPS rises with inflation, offering a safeguard for your investment.
- Real Estate: Investing in real estate can also serve as a hedge against inflation. Property values and rental incomes typically rise with inflation, providing an appreciating asset and a source of increasing income.

- Dividend-Growing Stocks: Companies with a history of increasing dividends can offer a double advantage. Not only do they provide an income that potentially rises over time, but they also represent ownership in businesses that may be able to pass on inflationary costs to consumers, thereby preserving their profit margins and your investment's value.
- Commodities: Direct investment in commodities like gold or oil or through commodity-focused funds can provide a buffer against inflation. Since commodity prices often rise with inflation, they can offer a counterbalance to the depreciating purchasing power of cash holdings.

Budget Adjustments

An adaptable budget is your frontline defense in maintaining financial stability amid inflation. Regularly revisiting and tweaking your budget can ensure that your spending aligns with the current cost of living. Some steps include:

- Annual Review: Conduct an annual review of your expenses, comparing them to the previous year's, to identify significant changes and adjust your budget accordingly.
- Discretionary Spending: Evaluate your discretionary spending with an eye toward flexibility. Recognizing areas where you can cut back or redirect funds can free up resources for essential expenses that may have increased due to inflation.
- Fixed Income Adjustments: For those with fixed retirement incomes, exploring options to supplement your income can be beneficial. Part-time work, freelancing, or turning a hobby into a source of income can provide additional financial cushioning.

Staying Informed

Staying abreast of economic trends and forecasts enables you to anticipate and react to inflationary pressures. Financial news outlets, economic reports, and advisories from financial institutions can offer valuable insights into inflation trends and their potential impact on your retirement savings. Moreover, engaging with a financial advisor who can monitor these trends and suggest timely adjustments to your investment strategy can be invaluable. They can provide personalized advice tailored to your financial situation, helping you navigate inflation's challenges with informed, strategic decisions.

Inflation poses a subtle yet significant threat to the purchasing power of your retirement savings. Understanding the risks it presents, adopting investment strategies that offer protection, making thoughtful budget adjustments, and staying informed about economic trends can effectively shield your finances from inflation's erosive effects. This proactive approach ensures that your retirement savings endure and thrive, supporting the comfortable, fulfilling retirement you've worked so hard to achieve.

11.3 ADJUSTING YOUR INVESTMENT STRATEGY IN VOLATILE MARKETS

In retirement planning, navigating the seas of market volatility requires a map and a compass to guide you through the ebbs and flows of economic tides. The strategies you employ to manage your investments are pivotal in ensuring financial stability, especially when the waters get rough. Here, we explore the nuances of crafting a resilient investment approach in the face of uncertainty.

Embracing a Long-term Perspective on Investments

Adopting a long-term viewpoint is one of the first steps to mitigate the stress of market fluctuations. Though often dramatic, short-term market movements tend to smooth out over the long haul. This perspective encourages patience and restraint from making hasty decisions based on temporary downturns. It's akin to watching the horizon while sailing: the immediate waves might be choppy, but your focus remains on the distant, steady line where the sky meets the sea. Keeping your eyes on the long-term goals makes it easier to ride out short-term volatility without veering off course.

Diversification as a Defense

Diversification acts as your portfolio's bulwark, a defensive strategy that spreads investments across various asset classes to reduce exposure to any single risk. It's the investment equivalent of not putting all your eggs in one basket. Suppose one sector or asset class takes a hit. In that case, the impact on your overall portfolio is cushioned by the performance of others. Effective diversification might include a mix of stocks, bonds, real estate, and cash, with further diversification within each category. This approach doesn't guarantee against loss but can significantly dampen the impact of market volatility.

Rebalancing Your Portfolio

Over time, the initial asset allocation in your portfolio can drift due to varying investments' performances. Rebalancing is the process of realigning the weightings of assets in your portfolio back to their target allocation. This might involve selling off investments that have grown beyond their desired proportion and purchasing more of those that have diminished. For instance, if your target allocation was 60% stocks and 40% bonds, and due to market gains, your stocks now represent 70% of your portfolio, you would sell some stocks and buy bonds to rebalance. This disciplined approach ensures that your portfolio maintains its intended risk profile, which is crucial for long-term investment success.

Seeking Professional Advice

In times of market uncertainty, the guidance of a seasoned financial advisor can be invaluable. They possess the expertise to analyze market conditions, suggest adjustments to your investment strategy, and offer reassurance when doubt creeps in. A professional can help you stay disciplined, reminding you of your financial goals and how your current strategy aligns with achieving them. They can also provide insights into new investment opportunities you might not have considered, further enhancing your portfolio's resilience against volatility.

Financial markets are inherently unpredictable, but you can confidently navigate their uncertainties with a well-thought-out investment strategy. Adopting a long-term perspective helps maintain focus on your retirement goals, diversification provides a buffer against market downturns, regular rebalancing ensures your portfolio stays aligned with your risk tolerance, and seeking professional advice can offer clarity and direction. These strategies together forge a path through volatile markets, securing your financial foundation for the years ahead.

As we wrap up this exploration of adjusting your investment strategy in volatile markets, it's clear that a thoughtful, disciplined approach is vital to maintaining financial equilibrium. The strategies discussed here shield your retirement savings from market fluctuations and position you to capitalize on growth opportunities. With these principles in mind, you're well-equipped to face the financial challenges and opportunities that lie ahead, ensuring your retirement years are as rewarding and secure as you've envisioned. Now, let's turn our attention to the next chapter, where we'll delve into the importance of staying healthy and active, ensuring that your retirement is financially sound and rich in well-being and vitality.

EMBRACING TECHNOLOGY FOR A RICHER RETIREMENT

I n a world where technology evolves at breakneck speed, staying in tune with the latest tools and apps can significantly enhance the quality of your retirement life. Far from being just gadgets and gizmos, technology offers practical solutions that can simplify financial management, boost your health, foster continuous learning, and even enrich your travel experiences. This chapter highlights how retirees can leverage technology to keep up with the times and thrive in their golden years.

Financial Management Tools

In the age of smartphones and tablets, managing your finances has never been easier, thanks to a plethora of apps and online tools designed to keep your retirement savings on track. Here's how technology can serve as your financial ally:

- Budgeting Apps: Apps like Mint and You Need A Budget (YNAB) can simplify tracking your spending and savings. With features like automatic expense categorization and personalized budget suggestions, these tools make it easy to see where your money goes and how to optimize your spending.

- Investment Tracking: Tools like Personal Capital offer a bird's-eye view of your assets for those with a portfolio of investments. You can monitor your investments' performance in real time, making it easier to adjust your strategy as needed.
- Bill Pay and Financial Alerts: Gone are the days of missed payments or overlooked due dates. Set up automatic bill payments and alerts for upcoming expenses to ensure your financial obligations are met without a hitch.

Incorporating these tools into your daily routine can save time and provide peace of mind, knowing that your finances are organized and under control.

Health and Fitness Apps

Maintaining a healthy lifestyle is crucial in retirement, and technology offers an array of apps to keep you on track:

- Exercise Apps: Whether you prefer yoga, strength training, or cardio, there's an app to guide your workout routine. Many offer customizable plans based on your fitness level and goals, complete with instructional videos.
- Diet and Nutrition Trackers: Apps like MyFitnessPal make it easy to log your daily food intake and monitor your nutritional goals. Tracking what you eat can help maintain a balanced diet and support your overall health.
- Meditation and Mindfulness: For mental well-being, meditation apps such as Headspace provide guided sessions to help reduce stress and improve sleep quality. Making meditation a regular part of your routine can enhance mental clarity and emotional balance.

Adopting these apps can motivate you to stay active and mindful, contributing to a healthier and more vibrant retirement.

Lifelong Learning Platforms

Retirement is an excellent time to explore new interests or deepen your knowledge in a favorite subject. Here's where technology comes in:

- Online Courses: Platforms like Coursera and Udemy offer courses on virtually every topic imaginable, from photography to philosophy. Many universities also provide free or low-cost access to their courses, making higher education more accessible than ever.
- Language Learning Apps: Are you dreaming of learning Italian or brushing up on your Spanish? Apps like Duolingo and Babbel make language learning fun and interactive, preparing you for your next overseas adventure.
- Creative Skills: For those interested in exploring their creative side, sites like Skillshare feature courses in drawing, writing, music, and more taught by experts in the field.

With these platforms, the joy of learning is literally at your fingertips, offering endless opportunities to grow and engage your mind.

Travel and Leisure Apps

For retirees bitten by the travel bug, technology can vastly simplify the planning and execution of your adventures:

- Travel Planning Apps: Apps like TripIt can organize your travel itinerary in one place, from flight details to hotel reservations and activities.
- Deal Finders: To stretch your travel budget further, apps such as Hopper predict flight and hotel price trends and alert you

when prices drop.

- Local Exploration: Once you're at your destination, apps like Google Maps and Yelp can help you discover local attractions, restaurants, and hidden gems, making your travels richer and more exciting.

Embracing these apps makes travel less stressful and more enjoyable, allowing you to focus on the experience rather than the logistics.

When wielded wisely, technology can significantly enhance the retirement experience. From managing your finances with ease to staying healthy, continuously learning, and traveling with confidence, the digital world offers tools and resources that cater to nearly every aspect of retired life. Integrating these technological solutions into your daily routine allows you to enjoy a simpler, more organized, richer, and more fulfilling retirement.

12.1 AUTOMATING YOUR SAVINGS AND INVESTMENTS

In financial management during retirement, ensuring a steady growth of your savings and investments without the daily hassle is a significant advantage. Automation stands out as a beacon of efficiency, offering a streamlined approach to securing your financial future. This segment delves into the myriad benefits of automation in savings and investments, guides you through setting up automatic transfers, introduces the concept of robo-advisors, and underscores the importance of keeping a watchful eye on these automated systems.

Benefits of Automation

The decision to automate your savings and investment contributions is akin to planting a garden that flourishes almost independently, with minimal regular upkeep. Here's why automation is a smart choice:

- Consistency: By setting up automatic contributions, you're committing to a consistent investment plan. This consistency is crucial in building wealth over time, adhering to the 'pay yourself first' principle.
- Simplicity: Once established, automated contributions relieve you of the need to manually transfer funds each month. This simplicity translates to more time enjoying retirement and less time managing finances.
- Emotional Detachment: Market fluctuations can tempt even the savviest investors into making impulsive decisions. Automation helps maintain your investment strategy unaffected by market volatility or emotional biases.
- Compounding Benefits: Regular, automated investments allow you to capitalize on the power of compounding interest, significantly impacting your savings growth over time.

Setting up Automatic Transfers

The process of setting up automatic transfers to your savings and investment accounts is straightforward, yet it requires careful planning:

1. Assessment: First, assess your monthly budget to determine a realistic and sustainable amount you can commit to saving and investing after covering living expenses.
2. Instructions: Log into your bank's online platform or visit in person to set up automatic transfers. You'll specify the amount, the accounts from which and to which the money will be transferred, and the frequency of transfers.
3. Coordination: If you have multiple savings or investment accounts, consider how to distribute your contributions to align with your financial goals, such as retirement savings, emergency funds, or specific investment portfolios.

Automated Investment Services

Robo-advisors represent a fusion of technology and investment management, offering a hands-off approach to managing your portfolio:

- Tailored Portfolios: After you input information regarding your financial goals and risk tolerance, robo-advisors create a personalized investment portfolio typically composed of low-cost index funds or ETFs.
- Rebalancing: These services automatically adjust your portfolio to maintain your desired asset allocation, ensuring your investments stay aligned with your objectives and risk level.
- Accessibility: Robo-advisors are generally more accessible than traditional investment advisors. They often require lower minimum investments and charge lower fees, making them an attractive option for retirees looking to optimize their investment strategy.

Monitoring Automated Systems

While automation in savings and investments offers convenience and efficiency, it is not a 'set it and forget it' solution. Active monitoring ensures these automated strategies continue to serve your best interests:

- Regular Reviews: Schedule periodic reviews of your automated savings contributions and investment allocations. This is especially important in retirement when your financial situation or goals may evolve.
- Performance Checks: Keep an eye on the performance of your investments, especially those managed by robo-advisors. Ensure they are performing as expected, and adjust your strategy if necessary.

- Fee Analysis: Regularly assess the fees associated with automated investment services. Over time, even small fees can eat into your returns, so it pays to stay informed and consider alternatives if fees become too burdensome.

By embracing automation in your financial management strategy, you can enjoy a more streamlined and stress-free approach to growing your retirement savings. However, remember that automation does not replace the need for periodic personal oversight. Staying engaged with your financial strategy ensures that your automated systems remain aligned with your evolving retirement goals, allowing you to make the most of your golden years.

12.2 STAYING INFORMED: FINANCIAL NEWS AND RESOURCES FOR RETIREES

In the golden years of retirement, staying abreast of the latest financial news and trends is not just about keeping busy; it's about safeguarding your financial future. This era of your life should be marked by wisdom, not just in how you spend your time but also in how you manage your resources. With the right approach to consuming financial news and leveraging online communities, you can ensure your retirement planning remains current and effective.

Curating a Personalized Financial News Feed

The digital age brings abundant information, but not all is beneficial or relevant to your needs. Creating a personalized financial news feed allows you to filter out the noise and focus on what truly matters for your retirement planning. Here's how to do it:

- Start by identifying your main interests and concerns. Are you keen on learning more about investment strategies, tax planning, or the latest in retirement living options?

Pinpointing your focus areas will guide your selection of news sources.

- Use news aggregator apps such as Feedly or Flipboard. These apps let you subscribe to various publications and organize articles into categories or 'feeds' based on your interests.
- Remember to include local news sources. They often provide vital information on state-specific tax laws or retirement benefits that national news might overlook.
- Finally, adjust your subscriptions as your interests or financial goals evolve. Your news feed should grow and change with you.

Reliable Financial News Sources

Discerning which sources to trust is crucial with the vast selection of financial news available. Here are some recommendations for reliable financial news outlets known for their accurate reporting and insightful analysis:

- The Wall Street Journal and The Financial Times are renowned for their comprehensive coverage of financial markets, economic policy, and personal finance.
- Bloomberg offers up-to-the-minute market data, news, and analysis, making it invaluable for those keeping a close eye on their investments.
- Forbes and Kiplinger provide accessible articles on retirement planning, investment strategies, and financial advice tailored to a non-professional audience.
- Always cross-reference news from multiple sources to get a well-rounded view and verify the accuracy of the information.

When evaluating financial information, consider the source's reputation, the author's credentials, and whether the content is fact-based or opinion-driven. This critical approach ensures you base your financial decisions on reliable information.

Online Communities for Retirees

The wisdom of a community can be a powerful tool in navigating the complexities of retirement planning. Online forums and communities offer a platform for retirees to share experiences, advice, and support. Websites like Reddit have subreddits dedicated to retirement and personal finance, where members actively discuss and share insights. Similarly, the Bogleheads forum, inspired by the investment philosophy of John Bogle, founder of Vanguard, provides a wealth of knowledge on low-cost investing, a crucial aspect of retirement planning. Engaging in these communities allows you to learn from the experiences of others, ask questions, and even offer guidance based on your journey.

Continuing Financial Education

The pursuit of knowledge should never cease, especially in retirement. Thankfully, the digital era makes continuing your financial education more accessible than ever. Here are some ways to keep learning:

- Webinars and Virtual Conferences: Many financial institutions and educational platforms host webinars covering investment strategies and estate planning topics. These sessions often allow for live Q&A, giving you the chance to have your questions answered by experts.
- Podcasts: Financial podcasts can be a great way to absorb information while on the go. Look for podcasts that focus on retirement planning and personal finance. They can be a source of both education and inspiration.
- Online Courses: Platforms such as Coursera and edX offer courses taught by university professors on economics, personal finance, and more. Many of these courses are free or low-cost.

Consuming financial news, engaging with online communities, and seeking educational opportunities ensures you remain informed and proactive about retirement management. This approach helps protect your financial well-being and enriches your retirement life with continuous learning and growth.

With these strategies for staying informed, you're better equipped to navigate the ever-changing landscape of retirement planning. By curating a personalized news feed, relying on reputable sources, engaging in online communities, and pursuing ongoing education, you're taking active steps to ensure your retirement strategy remains robust and responsive to the world around you. As we move forward, let's carry this spirit of informed engagement into all aspects of our retirement journey, from managing our health to exploring new passions.

13

THE ANNUAL RETIREMENT PLAN HEALTH CHECK

I magine your retirement plan as a garden you've meticulously cared for over the years. Just as gardens require regular tending, fertilization, and sometimes a bit of pruning to flourish, so does your retirement plan to ensure it sustains and nourishes you through the years ahead. An annual review of your retirement plan is not unlike this careful gardening, where examination and adjustments ensure your financial well-being continues to bloom.

13.1 HOW TO CONDUCT AN ANNUAL RETIREMENT PLAN REVIEW

Setting a Review Schedule

Marking your calendar for a regular annual review of your retirement plan can be as habitual as changing batteries in smoke detectors or scheduling a yearly physical—necessary tasks that maintain the health and safety of your household and yourself. The end of the year, or the beginning, often serves as an ideal time for this review, providing a natural pause to reflect on the past year and plan for the next.

However, aligning this review with significant personal milestones or tax deadlines can also offer practical benefits, ensuring your plan remains responsive to your current life stage and financial landscape.

Assessing Financial Performance

The first step in this annual review involves a close look at the performance of your investments versus your expectations and the market as a whole. It's like comparing this year's harvest to those of years past, understanding which crops (investments) thrived, which didn't, and why. This evaluation should cover:

- Returns on investments: How did your stocks, bonds, mutual funds, or other assets perform? Did they meet, exceed, or fall short of the market or the benchmarks you use for comparison?
- Fees and expenses: Have costs associated with managing your investments, such as account management fees or fund expense ratios, changed? High fees can eat into your returns over time.
- Asset allocation: Does the distribution of your investments across different asset classes still align with your risk tolerance and retirement timeline? Market movements can skew your original allocations, necessitating adjustments.

Tools like financial dashboards or consultations with a financial advisor can provide clarity and insight during this assessment, illuminating your portfolio's successes and areas for improvement.

Adjusting for Life Changes

Life is a river, constantly flowing and occasionally changing course. Significant life events—such as health changes, family dynamics shifting, or even relocating—necessitate a review and possible adjustment of your retirement plan. This part of the review ensures your plan remains tailored to your current circumstances. For example, a new health diagnosis may lead to increased medical expenses, requiring a reallocation of funds to cover these costs. Alternatively, a change in marital status might prompt a revision of your beneficiary designations or a re-evaluation of your long-term financial needs and goals.

Seeking Professional Advice

Sometimes, the best course of action involves seeking guidance from those who navigate these waters daily. A financial advisor can offer an objective perspective on your retirement plan, helping you make informed adjustments based on your financial performance review and any life changes. They can also provide insights into strategies you might not have considered, such as tax optimization techniques or new investment opportunities. It's like having a seasoned gardener advise you on how to rejuvenate your garden, offering tips on what to prune, plant anew, and protect against pests (or financial pitfalls).

Visual Element: Your Retirement Plan Review Checklist

An infographic checklist can visually guide you through the essential steps of conducting your annual retirement plan review. This checklist could include:

- Confirm the review date on your calendar.
- Gather necessary financial documents and statements.
- Assess the performance of your investments.
- Evaluate your current asset allocation.
- Reflect on any significant life changes in the past year.
- Decide if a consultation with a financial advisor is needed.
- Plan adjustments to your retirement strategy.

Interactive Element: Reflection on Changes

An interactive online questionnaire prompts you to reflect on any significant changes over the past year that could impact your retirement plan. Questions might cover health, family, housing, and hobbies, providing a structured way to consider how these changes intersect with your financial planning.

Textual Element: Real-Life Adjustments and Adaptations

A section is dedicated to sharing anonymized case studies of how individuals have successfully adjusted their retirement plans in response to life changes and financial performance. This segment can offer practical examples and inspiration for readers facing similar situations, showing how flexibility and proactive planning can keep retirement goals on track despite life's unpredictability.

By embracing the annual review of your retirement plan as a vital practice, you ensure that your financial well-being remains aligned with your evolving life circumstances and goals. This diligent attention to your financial garden helps secure the nourishment and growth of your retirement savings, allowing you to enjoy the fruits of your labor in the coming years.

13.2 WHEN LIFE CHANGES: ADAPTING YOUR RETIREMENT PLAN

Life's only constant is change, and this truth doesn't pause during our retirement years. Significant transformations in our health status, family structure, living situations, or financial state can unexpectedly alter the landscape of our meticulously planned retirement. Recognizing and adapting to these shifts is not just prudent; it's necessary for maintaining the security and happiness we aspire to in our later years.

Navigating Health Changes

Health changes rank among the most impactful events in retirement, affecting not just quality of life but also financial stability. Adapting your retirement plan to accommodate these changes involves several key strategies:

- Re-evaluating healthcare coverage: As health needs evolve, so do your healthcare coverage requirements. Consider supplemental health insurance plans or long-term care insurance to mitigate new or increased health-related expenses.
- Adjusting your budget: Increased medical costs may require adjusting your monthly budget. This could mean allocating more funds to healthcare and reducing non-essential spending.
- Exploring healthcare savings accounts: For those eligible, health savings accounts (HSAs) offer a tax-advantaged way to save for future medical expenses. Contributions are tax-deductible, and funds can be withdrawn tax-free for qualifying medical expenses, making HSAs a valuable tool in managing health-related financial changes.

Dealing with Family Dynamics

Family transitions, be they joyous or challenging, necessitate thoughtful adjustments to your retirement plan:

- Marriage or divorce: These significant relationship changes can lead to adjustments in your financial planning, beneficiary designations, and estate planning documents.
- Supporting family members: The need to financially support aging parents or adult children can emerge unexpectedly, requiring a careful reassessment of your budget and savings strategy. Creating a separate fund can help manage these

additional expenses without compromising your retirement savings.

- Inheritance considerations: Receiving or leaving an inheritance can significantly impact your financial landscape. Receiving an inheritance might offer new opportunities for investment or charitable giving. In planning to leave an inheritance, one might pursue detailed estate planning and discussions with financial advisors and family members.

Relocation Considerations

Relocating in retirement, whether for lifestyle preferences or cost of living adjustments, carries with it a host of considerations:

- Cost of living changes: Moving to a new area can either alleviate or increase financial strain depending on the cost of living differences. Researching and planning for these changes is crucial in ensuring your retirement savings can support your desired lifestyle in a new location.
- Tax implications: Different locales come with varying tax burdens. Some states offer tax benefits for retirees, such as no state income tax or exemptions on retirement income, which can influence your relocation decision.
- Social network impact: Moving can also affect your social connections and support network. Building new relationships and finding community in a new place are essential for maintaining emotional well-being in retirement.

Unexpected Financial Setbacks

Even the best-laid plans can be upended by unforeseen financial challenges. Here's how to handle unexpected setbacks without derailing your retirement:

- Emergency fund: Maintaining an emergency fund is a critical buffer against sudden financial needs. Ideally, this fund should cover several months of living expenses and be easily accessible.
- Revisiting investment strategies: A significant market downturn can impact your retirement savings. Consulting with a financial advisor to reassess your investment approach may help mitigate losses and reallocate assets more conservatively if nearing or in retirement.
- Reducing discretionary spending: Temporarily adjusting your lifestyle and spending habits can help you manage financial setbacks. Prioritizing essential expenses and finding cost-saving measures can make a significant difference.
- Income supplementation: In some cases, supplementing your income through part-time work, freelancing, or tapping into a hobby that can generate income may be necessary. This provides a financial cushion and adds structure and social engagement to your days.

Life changes, both expected and unexpected, are a natural part of the retirement landscape. By staying attuned to these shifts and ready to adjust your plans, you can ensure that your retirement remains as fulfilling and secure as you envisioned, regardless of twists and turns.

13.3 STAYING FLEXIBLE: THE KEY TO A SUCCESSFUL RETIREMENT

Flexibility in retirement planning is akin to navigating a ship through unpredictable seas. Conditions can change swiftly, and the ability to adjust your course is vital to reaching your destination safely. This section explores the essence of staying adaptable in life's inevitable shifts, ensuring your retirement remains rewarding and secure.

Embracing Change

Life's constant evolution demands we remain open to change, not just as an inevitability but as an opportunity for growth and enrichment. This mindset is particularly crucial in retirement, a period marked by significant transitions. Embracing change means viewing each new phase not with apprehension but as a chance to enhance your life's tapestry. It's about recognizing that the most well-thought-out plans may need revision as circumstances evolve. Therefore, remaining flexible allows you to easily navigate life's surprises, ensuring your retirement plan continues to serve your needs and aspirations.

Incorporating Flexibility in Financial Planning

A solid financial plan is the backbone of a secure retirement. However, true strength lies not in rigidity but in the capacity to adapt. Here are strategies to weave flexibility into your financial planning:

- Diversified Portfolio: An investment portfolio that spans various asset classes can better absorb market fluctuations, providing a steady course through economic storms. Consider a mix of stocks, bonds, real estate, and commodities to protect your financial well-being against different types of risk.
- Emergency Fund: Life has a way of presenting unexpected expenses, from home repairs to healthcare costs. An emergency fund is a financial cushion, ensuring you can cover these surprises without disrupting your retirement savings. Aim to have funds to cover several months of living expenses, and review this amount periodically to ensure it matches your current lifestyle needs.
- Adjustable Budget: An adaptable budget is vital. Regular reviews allow you to shift funds between categories as your priorities change, ensuring you allocate resources to what matters most at any given time. This might mean reallocating

entertainment funds to healthcare costs or vice versa, depending on your current phase of life.

Psychological Adaptability

Adapting to change isn't just a financial strategy; it's a state of mind. How you perceive and react to change can significantly impact your happiness and well-being in retirement. Cultivating a positive outlook on life's transitions can transform challenges into adventures and uncertainty into opportunity. Here are ways to foster psychological adaptability:

- Stay Curious: Approach new experiences with curiosity rather than apprehension. This can lead to discovering new passions and joys in retirement.
- Build Resilience: Reflect on past challenges you've overcome. This reflection can strengthen your resilience, reminding you that you have the skills and resources to handle future changes.
- Seek Support: A strong social network can provide emotional support and advice when navigating life's changes. Don't hesitate to lean on friends, family, or professionals for guidance.

Learning from Experience

Every change, challenge, or success in your life offers valuable lessons. Reflecting on these experiences provides insights that can guide future decisions, making you more adept at navigating the twists and turns of retirement. Consider keeping a journal to document or share these reflections with loved ones. This practice not only aids in personal growth but can also offer guidance and encouragement to others on their retirement journey.

In closing, the path to a fulfilling and secure retirement is marked by adaptability. By embracing change, incorporating flexibility into your financial planning, maintaining a positive outlook, and learning from experience, you can confidently navigate whatever the future holds. This approach ensures your retirement is not just a final chapter but a continuing story of growth, discovery, and joy. As we move forward, let's carry these principles, ready to adapt, grow, and thrive no matter what lies ahead.

14

THE EARLY EXIT: ASSESSING YOUR READINESS FOR EARLY RETIREMENT

In a world where the concept of retirement is often painted with broad strokes of leisurely days sans work-related stress, the allure of early retirement can be particularly strong. The dream of reclaiming one's time while still in the prime of life is a potent one. Yet, the shift from a structured work life to the freedom of early retirement is akin to stepping off a well-trodden path into uncharted territory. This chapter focuses on the multi-faceted assessment necessary to determine if early retirement is not just a desirable option but a viable one.

Financial Readiness

Determining financial readiness for early retirement is akin to planning an extended trip. Just as you would estimate costs, save money, and possibly consider income sources while traveling, early retirement planning follows a similar blueprint. Here's a breakdown of what to consider:

- Savings: Evaluate your current savings. Do they align with the 4% rule, which suggests you can comfortably withdraw 4% of your savings annually without depleting your nest egg prematurely? Though a helpful starting point, this rule may need adjustments based on your expected lifestyle and inflation.

- Investment Income: Assess your investments' ability to generate income. Stocks, bonds, and real estate can provide streams of income that supplement your savings. Consider whether these sources are reliable and can adjust for inflation over time.
- Healthcare Costs: With early retirement, employer-sponsored healthcare is often no longer an option. Calculating potential healthcare costs before Medicare eligibility at 65 is crucial. Marketplace insurance or health savings accounts (HSAs) can bridge the gap. Still, they come with their own costs and considerations.

Emotional Readiness

The emotional landscape of early retirement is vast and varied. It's not just about leaving a job; it's about entering a new phase of life. Here's what to reflect on:

- Leaving Your Career: Consider how your career influences your identity and social interactions. Stepping away from work means finding new ways to fulfill these aspects of your life.
- Finding Purpose and Fulfillment: Consider how you'll spend your days. Volunteering, hobbies, or part-time work provide structure and a sense of purpose. Reflect on what brings you joy and how you can integrate these activities into your daily life.

Lifestyle Considerations

Lifestyle changes that accompany early retirement are significant. They touch upon how you live, who you spend time with, and how you manage your day-to-day life. Key considerations include:

- Daily Structure: Without the work routine, your days might feel unmoored. Planning how you'll structure your time can help transition into early retirement smoothly. Will you adopt new hobbies? How will you ensure social interactions remain a part of your life?
- Living Arrangements: Early retirement might offer the chance to relocate. Whether downsizing or moving to a dream location, consider how your living situation fits into your retirement plan. Consider the cost of living, proximity to healthcare facilities, and opportunities for social engagement in your chosen location.

Risk Assessment

With early retirement comes a unique set of risks, primarily financial but also emotional and social. Here's how to evaluate and mitigate these risks:

- Longevity Risk: The possibility of outliving your savings is a real concern. Strategies like annuities or a more conservative withdrawal rate can help manage this risk.
- Market Volatility: Early retirement means your savings must last longer, making them more susceptible to market downturns. A well-diversified investment portfolio and a flexible withdrawal strategy can help navigate this volatility.
- Social and Emotional Risks: Losing social connections and a sense of purpose can impact well-being. Actively maintaining friendships and pursuing interests that provide fulfillment are vital.

Visual Element: Early Retirement Readiness Checklist

A checklist that helps you assess your readiness for early retirement, covering financial, emotional, and lifestyle considerations. This tool can be a practical guide in evaluating your current situation against the requirements of early retirement.

Interactive Element: Are You Ready for Early Retirement? Quiz

This online quiz asks you a series of questions about your financial situation, emotional state, and lifestyle preferences to help gauge your readiness for early retirement. The results can offer insights into areas where you may need to focus more on planning and preparation.

Textual Element: Case Studies on Early Retirement

Real-life examples of individuals who successfully transitioned into early retirement: These stories can highlight strategies to overcome challenges and provide a more nuanced understanding of early retirement.

Assessing your readiness for early retirement requires a comprehensive look at your financial health, emotional state, and lifestyle expectations. It's about making sure your savings can support you, you're prepared for the emotional shifts, and you have a clear vision of how you want to spend your early retirement years. Through careful planning and honest reflection, early retirement can be not just a dream but a rewarding and fulfilling chapter of your life.

14.1 UNDERSTANDING THE FIRE MOVEMENT

The Financial Independence Retire Early (FIRE) movement is more than just a trend; it's a shift in how we view work, life, and the concept of retirement itself. At its core, FIRE is about accumulating enough financial resources to allow you to retire much earlier than traditional retirement age. This doesn't necessarily mean leaving work altogether but having the financial security to choose work on your terms.

Variations of FIRE, such as "lean FIRE," where individuals live frugally to retire sooner, and "fat FIRE," which involves saving more for a more comfortable retirement lifestyle, reflect the diversity within the movement. Each path to FIRE is unique and tailored to individual ambitions, lifestyles, and definitions of financial independence.

Maximizing Savings Rates

Central to achieving FIRE is the ability to maximize your savings rate – the percentage of your income that you save and invest. Here are strategies to significantly increase this rate:

- Budget Optimization: Scrutinize your current spending to identify areas where you can cut back without sacrificing quality of life. This might involve swapping costly subscriptions for free alternatives or choosing more budget-friendly travel options.
- Increasing Income: Look for opportunities to boost your income, whether pursuing promotions, taking on freelance work, or starting a side business. Every additional dollar earned is another step closer to FIRE.
- Reducing Expenses: Examine your most significant expenses, such as housing, transportation, and food. Minor adjustments, like cooking at home more often or choosing a less expensive car, can significantly impact your savings rate over time.

Investment Strategies for FIRE

Investing wisely is just as critical as saving when it comes to achieving FIRE. It's about making your money work for you, generating passive income that grows over time. Here are key strategies:

- Low-Cost Index Funds: These funds mimic the performance of market indexes like the S&P 500 and come with lower fees than actively managed funds. They're a favorite in the FIRE community for their simplicity and effectiveness over the long term.
- Real Estate: For those inclined towards tangible assets, real estate investments can provide both rental income and appreciation. This requires more hands-on management but can be a lucrative component of a FIRE strategy.
- Diversification: Spreading investments across different asset classes reduces risk and provides more stable returns. This might mean holding a mix of stocks, bonds, real estate, and even alternative investments like peer-to-peer lending.

Life After FIRE

Achieving financial independence opens up a new world of possibilities. However, managing your investments and ensuring financial security in early retirement requires careful planning:

- Withdrawal Strategy: Establish a sustainable withdrawal rate that allows your portfolio to last. Given the longer retirement horizon, this rate may need to be lower than the traditional 4% rule.
- Healthcare Planning: With early retirement comes the responsibility of securing healthcare coverage independently. Research your options well in advance, considering health-sharing plans, part-time work that offers benefits, or the healthcare marketplace.
- Ongoing Investment Management: Your investment strategy may shift in early retirement. Moving towards more conservative investments or rebalancing your portfolio to match your changing risk tolerance will help protect your nest egg.

- Finding Fulfillment: Retirement isn't just about financial independence; it's also about personal fulfillment. Many find joy in pursuing passions, volunteering, or even starting a new career or business venture. The key is to find activities that bring purpose and joy to your days.

Achieving FIRE isn't simply about reaching a financial milestone but redefining what retirement means to you. It's a personal journey that requires dedication, planning, and a bit of creativity. Whether you're aiming for lean FIRE, fat FIRE, or somewhere in between, the principles of maximizing savings, investing wisely, and planning for life after reaching your goal will guide you toward a future where work is optional and financial freedom is a reality.

14.2 HEALTHCARE AND INSURANCE BEFORE MEDICARE

Navigating the waters of healthcare before reaching Medicare eligibility presents a unique set of challenges for those considering early retirement. The safety net that comes with employment - employer-sponsored healthcare - disappears, leaving a gap that must be thoughtfully bridged to ensure uninterrupted and affordable healthcare coverage.

Healthcare Options

Several avenues exist for securing healthcare coverage prior to Medicare eligibility:

- Marketplace Insurance: The Affordable Care Act (ACA) marketplace offers a range of healthcare plans. These plans are categorized from bronze to platinum, reflecting their coverage levels and premium costs. Subsidies based on income can make these plans more affordable for early retirees.

- COBRA: The Consolidated Omnibus Budget Reconciliation Act allows you to extend your employer-provided health insurance for up to 18 months after leaving your job. While COBRA ensures continuity of coverage, it can be expensive since you'll be paying the full premium amount, including the portion previously covered by your employer.
- Health Sharing Plans: These are not insurance but rather cooperative healthcare plans where members share medical expenses. They often come with lower monthly costs but may have limitations on coverage, such as pre-existing conditions or specific types of healthcare services.

Cost Considerations

Understanding and planning for healthcare costs before Medicare kicks in is crucial. Here's how to manage these expenses effectively:

- Premiums: These are your monthly payments for healthcare coverage. Premiums vary widely based on the type of plan, coverage level, and geographic location. Shop and compare plans to find one that meets your needs and budget.
- Out-of-pocket expenses include deductibles, copayments, and coinsurance. High-deductible plans often have lower premiums but require more out-of-pocket expenses before insurance covers them. Balancing premiums with out-of-pocket costs is vital to finding a cost-effective strategy.
- Minimizing Costs: Strategies to reduce healthcare costs include choosing a plan that covers your regular medications and doctors, using in-network providers, and taking advantage of preventative care covered under the ACA.

Health Savings Accounts (HSAs)

HSAs offer a tax-advantaged way to save for healthcare expenses. Still, you must be enrolled in a high-deductible health plan to qualify.

Benefits include:

- Pre-tax Contributions: You can contribute to an HSA with pre-tax dollars, reducing your taxable income.
- Tax-Free Withdrawals: Funds withdrawn for qualified medical expenses are not taxed.
- Investment Growth: HSA funds can be invested, and any growth is tax-free, provided it's used for qualified medical expenses.
- No Expiry: Unlike Flexible Spending Accounts (FSAs), HSA funds roll over year to year and can be used in retirement.

HSAs can be a powerful tool for managing healthcare costs before Medicare, offering tax savings and flexibility.

Planning for Long-Term Care

Long-term care, not typically covered by Medicare, requires separate planning:

- Long-term care Insurance covers services like nursing home care, assisted living, or in-home care. Policies vary in coverage and cost, so shopping around and finding a policy that fits your needs and budget is essential.
- Hybrid Insurance Policies: Some life insurance policies include long-term care benefits, providing flexibility in how you use the policy.
- Savings and Investments: Setting aside a portion of your savings or investments specifically for potential long-term care expenses can also be a strategy, though it requires careful planning to ensure sufficient funds.

In closing, stepping into early retirement without the safety net of employer-sponsored healthcare demands careful planning and consideration. From exploring your options for coverage to understanding the nuances of HSAs and planning for long-term care, being well-informed will help you navigate this transition smoothly and ensure you're covered until Medicare begins. As we continue, we'll shift our focus to maintaining a healthy lifestyle, emphasizing the importance of physical well-being in enhancing the quality of retirement life.

15

LEGACY BEYOND WEALTH: MAKING A DIFFERENCE IN RETIREMENT

R etirement, often viewed through the lens of financial security and leisure, holds a more profound potential for impact—both in our lives and the wider community. This chapter shifts focus from the nuts and bolts of financial planning to the broader canvas of legacy. Here, legacy isn't just about assets; it's about influence, contribution, and the mark we leave on the world through philanthropy and charitable giving.

15.1 PHILANTHROPY AND CHARITABLE GIVING IN RETIREMENT

Identifying Causes and Organizations

At the heart of meaningful philanthropy lies a connection to the causes we care about. It's one thing to write a check; it's another to invest in a mission that resonates with our deepest values. Start by reflecting on the issues that stir you—whether it's education, environment, health, or social justice. Websites like GuideStar or Charity Navigator can help you vet organizations for their impact and financial health, ensuring your contributions go where they can do the most good.

Strategies for Charitable Giving

Philanthropy in retirement can take many forms, each with its own set of considerations:

- Direct Donations: The most straightforward way to support a cause. Scheduled giving, such as monthly donations, can consistently support your chosen organization.
- Donor-Advised Funds (DAFs): DAFs serve as philanthropic accounts, allowing you to make a charitable contribution, receive an immediate tax deduction, and then recommend grants from the fund over time. This can be an effective way to manage your charitable giving.
- Charitable Trusts: Setting up a charitable trust can offer tax benefits while supporting your philanthropic goals. A Charitable Remainder Trust (CRT), for example, can provide you with income during your lifetime, with the remainder going to your chosen charity upon your passing.
- Volunteering: Giving time can be as valuable as financial contributions. Many organizations rely on volunteers for day-to-day operations, offering a hands-on way to support a cause.

Tax Implications and Benefits

Charitable giving can offer tax advantages, potentially lowering your taxable income. For direct donations, keep detailed records of contributions for tax purposes. If you're considering a DAF or charitable trust, consult a financial advisor to understand the tax benefits and requirements. Remember, the goal is to make an impact while managing your financial health in retirement.

Volunteering and Non-Monetary Contributions

Beyond financial support, volunteering provides a direct way to contribute to the causes you care about. It also offers personal benefits, such as staying active, meeting new people, and learning new skills. Consider your skills and interests when seeking volunteer opportunities, and seek roles that offer personal fulfillment and community benefit.

Visual Element: Chart of Charitable Giving Strategies

An infographic outlines the different strategies for charitable giving in retirement, including direct donations, DAFs, charitable trusts, and volunteering. The chart highlights the benefits and considerations of each option, providing a visual guide to impactful giving.

Interactive Element: Philanthropy Values Exercise

A guided exercise to help you identify your philanthropic values and interests. This might include journaling prompts to explore what issues matter most to you and why, or a quiz that matches your interests with potential causes and organizations.

Textual Element: Real-Life Philanthropy Stories

This is a collection of stories from retirees who have found fulfillment and purpose through philanthropy and charitable giving. These narratives showcase the diverse ways individuals can make a difference, from local community projects to global initiatives, offering inspiration and practical ideas for your philanthropic journey.

Philanthropy and charitable giving in retirement open new avenues for leaving a lasting legacy. By aligning your charitable efforts with your values and utilizing strategic giving methods, you can ensure that your contributions have a lasting impact. Whether through financial donations, volunteering, or a combination of both, your retirement years offer a unique opportunity to give back and enrich both your life and the lives of others.

15.2 TEACHING FINANCIAL LITERACY TO FUTURE GENERATIONS

Financial literacy is a critical skill often overlooked in traditional education systems. As retirees, we hold a treasure trove of lived financial experiences that, when passed down, can empower our children and grandchildren to navigate their economic futures with confidence. This section explores how embedding financial education into our legacy can set the stage for future financially savvy generations.

The Importance of Financial Education

Financial literacy goes beyond understanding numbers on a spreadsheet; it's about making informed decisions that lead to a secure and fulfilling life. Teaching children and grandchildren the value of savings, the impact of investing, and the nuances of budgeting equips them with tools to achieve their dreams, be it higher education, homeownership, or entrepreneurial ventures. Moreover, it instills confidence to face financial challenges and opportunities head-on, ensuring they're prepared for economic ups and downs.

Effective Teaching Methods

Every age group absorbs information differently, demanding tailored approaches to financial education:

- For young children, storytelling can be a powerful tool. Use narratives around saving for a toy or planning a lemonade stand to introduce concepts of savings and cost.
- Teenagers often respond well to hands-on experiences. Consider setting up a mock stock portfolio or involving them

in family budgeting exercises to teach investment and money management.

- Adult children might benefit from deeper discussions on retirement planning, estate planning, and the importance of insurance. Sharing your experiences, both successes and missteps can provide valuable real-life context.

Incorporating technology can also enhance learning, with apps and online games designed to teach financial concepts in an engaging way. Encourage them to set financial goals and track progress, fostering a sense of ownership and responsibility towards their financial future.

Incorporating Financial Education into Estate Planning

Estate planning isn't just about distributing assets; it's an opportunity to pass on values and knowledge. Consider these strategies:

- Educational Trusts: Setting up a trust with stipulations for financial education can ensure heirs inherit assets and have the wisdom to manage them. For instance, funds could be released as beneficiaries reach certain educational milestones, such as completing a personal finance course.
- Resource Provision: Include financial education resources in your will or as part of trust distributions. This could be a collection of books, subscriptions to financial magazines, or memberships to financial advisory services.
- Family Meetings: Use estate planning discussions to engage family members in conversations about financial values, the importance of philanthropy, and the responsibilities that come with wealth. These meetings can serve as informal financial education sessions, fostering a culture of transparency and learning.

Leading by Example

Perhaps the most potent method of teaching financial literacy is to lead by example. Demonstrating sound financial management, the importance of regular savings, strategic investing, and philanthropy can leave a lasting impression. Let them see you budgeting, hear you discussing financial decisions openly, and watch you navigating financial challenges with grace. Actions often speak louder than words; your financial behavior is a continuous lesson in prudence and planning.

By embedding financial education into our legacy, we do more than pass on wealth; we empower future generations with the knowledge and skills to grow that wealth responsibly. This ensures the longevity of our financial legacies and contributes to our families' financial well-being for generations to come.

15.3 DOCUMENTING YOUR LIFE AND VALUES FOR POSTERITY

In the tapestry of life, each thread represents a story, lesson, or value that we've gathered along the way. As we consider the legacy we wish to leave behind, it becomes clear that our financial assets are only a part of the picture. Equally important, if not more so, are the stories, beliefs, and values that have shaped our journey. This section explores ways to ensure these intangible yet invaluable assets are passed on to future generations, enriching their lives and those beyond.

Creating a Personal Legacy Document

Imagine compiling a document that captures not just the milestones of your life but also the wisdom you've acquired, the values you hold dear, and the hopes you harbor for your loved ones. This is the essence of a personal legacy document. It's a way to share what you did, who you were, and what you believed in.

To create this document:

- Start with an outline that includes significant life events, lessons learned, values, and advice you wish to pass on.
- Include stories or anecdotes that illustrate these values in action. Perhaps a challenge you overcame that taught you resilience or a moment of failure that led to unexpected growth.
- Reflect on the advice you would have found useful at various stages of your life and share this with your future generations.

This document can evolve over time, growing richer as you continue to experience and reflect upon life.

Ethical Wills

Unlike a legal document, an ethical will is a heartfelt expression of what truly matters to you. It's an ancient practice, modernized to help you articulate your values, blessings, life's lessons, and hopes for the future.

To craft your ethical will:

- Consider the core values that have guided your life. What principles do you want to ensure live on after you're gone?
- Think about the hopes you have for your family's future. What wisdom can you share to help guide them on their path?
- Use simple, honest language. This is your voice speaking across generations, so let your true self shine through.

Ethical wills can be shared with your family while you're still alive, offering a profound opportunity for connection and understanding.

Oral Histories and Memoirs

Your life story is a unique narrative that holds lessons, joys, sorrows, and wisdom earned along the way. Capturing this story through oral histories or memoirs can be a precious gift to your family and future generations.

Consider these approaches:

- Audio recordings: Conversations about your life, captured digitally, offer a personal and intimate way for your descendants to know you. You might recount specific events, share stories of your ancestors, or discuss the values that have been important to you.
- Written memoirs: Writing your life story can be therapeutic, allowing you to reflect on your journey. Start with significant life events and expand by including the lessons learned and the values these experiences reinforced.

These narratives provide a personal connection that transcends time, allowing your essence and wisdom to be felt by generations to come.

Managing Your Digital Legacy

In today's digital age, our online presence is an extension of our lives, holding memories, conversations, and expressions of our interests and values. Managing this digital legacy is becoming increasingly important.

To ensure your digital legacy is handled according to your wishes:

- Make a list of your digital assets, including social media profiles, blogs, and digital photo libraries.
- Decide what should happen to these accounts and assets. Would you like them to be memorialized, passed on, or deleted?

- Use available tools provided by platforms (like Facebook's Legacy Contact) to ensure your wishes are carried out.
- Include instructions for your digital assets in your estate plan, providing access to accounts where necessary.

Your digital footprint is a part of your story. Managing it thoughtfully ensures that your online presence continues to reflect your wishes and values.

As we wrap up this chapter, it's clear that the legacy we leave encompasses far more than financial assets. The stories, values, and wisdom we impart can guide and inspire future generations, offering them a sense of connection and continuity. By documenting our life experiences, articulating our values through ethical wills, preserving our stories through oral histories and memoirs, and thoughtfully managing our digital legacy, we ensure that the essence of who we are lives on. As we move forward, let us embrace the opportunity to reflect on our lives, share our wisdom, and curate the legacy we leave behind, weaving a rich tapestry for those who follow in our footsteps.

HELP OTHERS BUILD UPON THEIR FINANCIAL STRENGTHS

I wrote this book to help readers understand that retirement isn't any harder than making any key life decision. The process starts within... the first step lies in identifying your values and the kind of retirement you wish to have. Once you know where you're at and where you would like to be, success involves taking a small but powerful list of steps that help you advance much quicker than you may have thought possible.

Throughout these pages, I have steered clear of a "one-size-fits-all" solution. For every key planning stage, I have offered you information and filled you in on the pros and cons of various strategies—so you can make the smartest decision for yourself. If this book has helped you ensure that no stone is left unturned, please leave a short review and let readers know that the perfect time to start planning is right now.

LEAVE A REVIEW!

Thanks for your help. Knowledge is something that is freely shared, yet brings such great returns. Through your words, you can inspire someone to take the reins of their financial future into their own hands.

Scan the QR code below

CONCLUSION

As we draw the curtains on this comprehensive journey that unfolded from the pages of laying your financial foundation to the intricate dance of adapting and thriving in your golden years, I find myself reflecting with immense gratitude and a sense of shared anticipation. You've navigated through the pivotal areas of retirement planning, from the initial steps in understanding and leveraging financial instruments to mastering the nuances of healthcare, Social Security, and the digital realm, all the way to the profound realms of estate and legacy planning.

The key takeaways from our exploration are manifold. Early and informed planning stands as the bedrock of a secure future. The magic of compounding interest, the shield of healthcare readiness, the strategic maneuvers around Social Security, and the thoughtful curation of your legacy—each plays a critical role in sculpting a retirement that's not just financially sound but also rich in purpose and fulfillment. Moreover, the embrace of technology has emerged as an indispensable ally in this endeavor.

However, if there's one principle that threads through the fabric of successful retirement planning, it is adaptability. The landscape of life is ever-shifting, and with it, our plans must evolve. A static strategy is a vulnerable one. Thus, the importance of regular reviews, recalibrations, and the readiness to pivot when the winds of change blow cannot be overstated.

Now, I extend a call to action, not as a command but as an invitation. This is an invitation to step into the arena of proactive planning, regardless of where you stand today in life's timeline. The strategies and insights shared within these pages are your tools—wield them with confidence, seek counsel from seasoned professionals when you encounter crossroads, and remain an active participant in crafting your retirement narrative.

The journey of learning is perpetual. I encourage you to keep your curiosity kindled, your knowledge base expanding, and your eyes open to the evolving economic landscapes and opportunities they herald. This is not merely about financial security; it's about empowering you to navigate the complexities of retirement planning with agility and optimism.

I recognize that the path is strewn with challenges, but within you lies the capacity to surmount them. This book aims to be a compass, guiding you through the mazes and over the mountains, equipping you with the clarity and confidence to forge ahead.

Your stories, experiences, and insights are invaluable. I invite you to share them and contribute to a tapestry of collective wisdom and learning. We can continue this conversation through a dedicated platform—a website or social media—building a community of empowered individuals journeying toward a fulfilling retirement.

And while this book might seem like a destination, it's merely a checkpoint. The landscape of retirement planning is vast and ever-evolving. Stay tuned for further resources, updates, and guides that will continue to build upon the foundation we've laid together.

In closing, I express my deepest gratitude for your trust and companionship through this exploration. Your engagement and thirst for knowledge have enriched this journey and reinforced my commitment to assisting you in achieving the retirement you envision and deserve.

Let's look forward to the unwritten chapters, the plans yet crafted, and the dreams yet realized. Thank you for allowing me the privilege of being a part of your journey to a secure and enriched retirement.

REFERENCES

Visualize Retirement: Retirement Planning Checklist https://www.troweprice.com/financial-intermediary/us/en/insights/articles/2021/q4/visualize-retirement-retirement-planning-checklist.html

Health Care Planning for Retirement https://www.wespath.org/health-well-being/health-well-being-resources/physical-well-being/healthcareplanningforretirement

What is financial flexibility and why is it so important? https://www.cnbc.com/select/what-is-financial-flexibility/

IRA vs. 401(k): How to Choose - NerdWallet https://www.nerdwallet.com/article/investing/ira-vs-401k-retirement-accounts#:

Roth IRA Contribution and Income Limits 2023-2024 https://www.nerdwallet.com/article/investing/roth-ira-contribution-limits#:

How to manage your retirement asset allocation https://www.fidelity.com/learning-center/personal-finance/retirement-asset-allocation

Taxation of Retirement Income | FINRA.org https://www.finra.org/investors/learn-to-invest/types-investments/retirement/managing-retirement-income/taxation-retirement-income#:

Why You Need To Do A Personal Financial Audit [+ How ... https://www.theconfusedmillennial.com/personal-financial-audit/

What's Your Net Worth Telling You? https://www.investopedia.com/articles/pf/08/ideal-net-worth.asp

6 Reasons You Need an Emergency Fund in Retirement https://getcarefull.com/articles/6-reasons-you-need-an-emergency-fund-in-retirement#:

Retirement Planning: A 5-Step Guide for 2024 https://www.nerdwallet.com/article/investing/retirement-planning-an-introduction

6 Reasons Why You Should Start Retirement Planning Early https://districtcapitalmanagement.com/start-retirement-planning-early/

Catch-Up Contribution: What It Is, How It Works, Rules, and ... https://www.investopedia.com/terms/c/catchupcontribution.asp

undefined undefined

How Much Will My Roth IRA Be Worth? Power of ... https://www.investopedia.com/one-day-your-roth-ira-will-fund-itself-4770849

Investment Diversification: What It Is and How To Do It https://www.nerdwallet.com/article/investing/diversification

How to Determine Your Risk Tolerance Level https://www.schwab.com/learn/story/how-to-determine-your-risk-tolerance-level

ETFs vs. Index Mutual Funds: What's the Difference? https://www.investopedia.com/articles/mutualfund/05/etfindexfund.asp

How to Rebalance Your Portfolio - Investopedia https://www.investopedia.com/how-to-rebalance-your-portfolio-7973806

Roth IRA vs. 401(k): What's the Difference? - Investopedia https://www.investopedia.com/ask/answers/100314/whats-difference-between-401k-and-roth-ira.asp

3 Strategies for Reducing Roth IRA Conversion Taxes https://www.schwab.com/learn/story/3-strategies-reducing-roth-ira-conversion-taxes

How Retirement Account Withdrawals Affect Your Tax ... https://www.investopedia.com/ask/answers/030316/do-retirement-account-withdrawals-affect-tax-brackets.asp

Tax Loss Harvesting: A Portfolio and Wealth Planning Perspective https://corporate.vanguard.com/content/dam/corp/research/pdf/Tax-Loss-Harvesting-A-Portfolio-and-Wealth-Planning-Perspective-US-ISGTLH_102020_online.pdf

How to Plan for Medical Expenses in Retirement https://www.investopedia.com/retirement/how-plan-medical-expenses-retirement/

How to Sign Up: A Guide to Medicare Enrollment https://www.aarp.org/health/medicare-insurance/info-2020/enrolling-in-medicare.html

Medicare Advantage vs. Medicare Supplement (Medigap) https://www.forbes.com/health/medicare/medicare-advantage-vs-medicare-supplement/

undefined undefined

How Social Security Benefits Are Calculated - Bankrate https://www.bankrate.com/retirement/how-social-security-benefits-are-calculated/

Determining The Best Age to Collect Social Security (for You) https://www.ml.com/articles/social-security-aiming-for-smarter-payments.html

Social Security Claiming Strategies for Couples https://www.aarp.org/retirement/social-security/info-2022/claiming-strategies-for-couples.html

Social Security Changes - COLA Fact Sheet https://www.ssa.gov/news/press/factsheets/colafacts2023.pdf

Estate Planning Basics https://www.fidelity.com/life-events/estate-planning/basics

How to choose an executor for your estate - TIAA https://www.tiaa.org/public/learn/life-milestones/how-to-choose-an-executor-for-your-estate

durable power of attorney | Wex - Law.Cornell.Edu https://www.law.cornell.edu/wex/durable_power_of_attorney

3 health benefits of volunteering https://www.mayoclinichealthsystem.org/hometown-health/speaking-of-health/3-health-benefits-of-volunteering

Lifelong Learning Opportunities for Older Adults and Retirees https://www.rightathome.net/blog/lifelong-learning-opportunities-for-older-adults-and-retirees

How to Plan for Travel in Retirement https://www.investopedia.com/retirement/how-plan-travel-retirement/

Participating in Activities You Enjoy As You Age https://www.nia.nih.gov/health/healthy-aging/participating-activities-you-enjoy-you-age

Adjusting to Retirement: Handling Depression and Stress https://www.helpguide.org/articles/aging-issues/adjusting-to-retirement.htm

How Retirees Can Protect Their Savings From High ... https://www.troweprice.com/personal-investing/resources/insights/how-retirees-can-protect-their-savings-from-rising-inflation.html

How to Rebalance Your Portfolio - Investopedia https://www.investopedia.com/how-to-rebalance-your-portfolio-7973806

How To Invest In Volatile Markets With A Financial Advisor https://www.forbes.com/advisor/investing/financial-advisor/how-to-invest-in-volatile-markets-with-a-financial-advisor/

Great Retirement Planning Tools and Software for 2023 https://money.usnews.com/money/retirement/401ks/articles/best-retirement-planning-tools-and-software

9 Ways To Automate Your Savings https://www.forbes.com/advisor/banking/savings/how-to-automate-your-savings/

Kiplinger | Personal Finance News, Investing Advice ... https://www.kiplinger.com/

30 Best Online Learning Platforms for 2024 https://www.learnworlds.com/online-learning-platforms/

8 Steps for Your Annual 401(k) Checkup https://www.kiplinger.com/slideshow/retirement/t001-s003-8-steps-for-your-annual-401-k-checkup/index.html

Managing Your Retirement Savings Through Life's Transitions https://www.alanet.org/legal-management/2018/february/departments/managing-your-retirement-savings-through-lifes-transitions

5 Retirement Planning Steps to Take https://www.investopedia.com/articles/retirement/11/5-steps-to-retirement-plan.asp

Facilitators and barriers for successful retirement https://www.ncbi.nlm.nih.gov/pmc/articles/PMC10237219/

Financial Independence, Retire Early (FIRE) Explained https://www.investopedia.com/terms/f/financial-independence-retire-early-fire.asp

Bridging the health care coverage gap https://www.fidelity.com/viewpoints/retirement/transition-to-medicare

How to Know When You're Financially Ready for Retirement https://www.accuplan.net/blog/financially-ready-for-retirement/

Financial Independence, Retire Early (FIRE) Explained https://www.investopedia.com/terms/f/financial-independence-retire-early-fire.asp

Charitable giving in retirement - Guardian Life https://www.guardianlife.com/charitable-giving

9 Tips for Teaching Kids About Money https://www.schwab.com/learn/story/9-tips-teaching-kids-about-money

How to Write a Legacy Statement - The Most Important Gift ... https://your-philanthropy.com/write-legacy-statement/

Managing Your Digital Legacy in 6 Steps | HealthNews https://healthnews.com/family-health/end-of-life-care/managing-your-digital-legacy-in-six-steps/

McGough, Nellah Bailey. "75 Retirement Quotes That Will Resonate With Any Retiree." Southern Living. April 25, 2024. https://www.southernliving.com/culture/retirement-quotes

www.ingramcontent.com/pod-product-compliance
Lightning Source LLC
Chambersburg PA
CBHW030520210326
41597CB00013B/978